CYPRUS

CYPRUS

An Ancient People,
a Troubled History, and
One Last Chance for Peace

**LAWRENCE STEVENSON &
GLYNNIS STEVENSON**

sh.
SUTHERLAND
HOUSE
TORONTO, 2021

Sutherland House
416 Moore Ave., Suite 205
Toronto, ON M4G 1C9

First edition, May 2022

If you are interested in inviting one of our authors to a live event or media appearance, please contact publicity@sutherlandhousebooks.com and visit our website at sutherlandhousebooks.com for more information about our authors and their schedules.

Manufactured in Canada
Cover designed by Lena Yang
Book composed by Karl Hunt

Library and Archives Canada Cataloguing in Publication
Title: Cyprus : an ancient people, a troubled history, and one last chance for peace / Lawrence & Glynnis Stevenson.
Names: Stevenson, Lawrence, author. | Stevenson, Glynnis, author.
Description: Includes bibliographical references.
Identifiers: Canadiana 20210388366 | ISBN 9781989555637 (hardcover)
Subjects: LCSH: Cyprus—History—Cyprus Crisis, 1974-
Classification: LCC DS54.9 .S74 2022 | DDC 956.9304—dc23

ISBN 978-1-989555-63-7

CONTENTS

INTRODUCTION

CYPRUS ENTERED MY LIFE in 1979, when as a young officer my battalion of the Princess Patricia's Canadian Light Infantry (PPCLI) was notified that we would be posted to Cyprus in 1980 for a six-month peacekeeping tour. Over several months, the battalion trained, was briefed, and read to ensure that we understood the situation in Cyprus. Hellenic culture has always been fascinating to me. In high school and college, I read and admired Thucydides, Homer, Byron, and studied the life of one of the all-time great politicians, Pericles. I was fascinated by the exploits of Alexander the Great and read about the Spartans, the Peloponnesian Wars and Thermopylae. The Turkish world was much less known to me. They were foreign and "other" to me based on limited knowledge that I had gleaned from my favourite film "Lawrence of Arabia" and from one of the popular films of that time, "Midnight Express." The latter chronicled the harrowing story of an American arrested in Turkey for drug possession. Any Westerner who saw or watched "Midnight Express" certainly was fearful of the Turks who were portrayed in the film, as cold and brutal.

The fascination with Greek culture and wariness about Turks led most of us to head to Cyprus with a bias in favour of the Greek-Cypriots. This bias was only amplified by the reading I did as I prepared for my peacekeeping tour. Most articles and books highlighted that the problem was caused essentially by the intransigence of the Turks and the Turkish-Cypriots and that most of the mess was caused by Turkey's unprovoked invasion of Cyprus in 1974. However, the 1974 invasion was anything other than unprovoked. The actions taken by the Greeks and the Greek-Cypriots in that fateful year led directly to the Turkish invasion. Contrary to the Greek-Cypriot storyline, the Turkish invasion in 1974 was not the beginning of this sorry tale.

The Greek-Cypriots would claim that the Turkish-Cypriots have no rights to the island but this ignores the fact that the Turks have been on the island for more than 400 years and that for three centuries they were masters of the island—the Ottoman Empire ruled Cyprus until the end of the nineteenth-century, despite being outnumbered by Greek-Cypriots. The Turks relinquished control of Cyprus to Britain in 1878 and over time the Turkish-Cypriots were increasingly marginalized and targeted by the majority Greek-Cypriots. British rule kept things in check but Cypriot independence in 1960 re-opened old wounds as both communities felt that the new constitution did not give them the powers they deserved. Greek-Cypriots would not abide by the minority rights that had been granted the Turkish-Cypriots, and in 1964 the Cypriot president, Archbishop Makarios, unilaterally abolished many of those enshrined rights which led to intensified inter-communal fighting. These escalated tensions eventually led to the introduction of UN peacekeeping forces in 1964, which kept the lid on the boiler until 1974. That year, the Greek military junta in Athens overthrew the Cypriot government with the objective of completely subjugating the Turkish-Cypriot minority and having Cyprus united with Greece, which was the ultimate dream of most Greek-Cypriots at the time.

A Greek-Cypriot coup overthrew President Makarios and put a murderous thug, Nicos Sampson, in charge of Cyprus. His stated objective was to rid the island of Turkish-Cypriots. The genocide he launched claimed many Turkish-Cypriot lives in the summer of 1974. In many villages the Turkish-Cypriot males were rounded up and never seen again. In one community, fourteen Turkish-Cypriot children were slaughtered, the youngest only four months old. These atrocities led directly to the Turkish army's intervention in the summer of 1974. This intervention by Turkey was specifically allowed, as they were a guarantor power in the 1960 Treaty that granted independence to Cyprus.

The Turkish invasion of 1974 certainly led to the division of the island that persists to this day, but it did not cause the Cyprus problem. As a young officer, my reading eventually led me to the conclusion that there was another side to this story overlooked by most Western observers. The Western bias was not helped by the fact that, as a UN peacekeeper, I socialized almost exclusively with Greek-Cypriots and seldom with Turkish-Cypriots. This was true of all the UN peacekeepers, who essentially lived their lives in Greek Cyprus with occasional forays to the Turkish-Cypriot side for either official business, quick tourist trips, or in my case for scuba diving excursions on the beautiful northern coast. We played soccer against the Greek-Cypriots and enjoyed their many fine restaurants in Nicosia. We Canadians lived in the Ledra Palace Hotel which at one time was the envy of the Levant. In 1980, it was no longer a gem, but it did offer us a swimming pool and tennis courts and a view of both sides of the protected green line in Nicosia. Our cook in the officers' mess was a wonderful Greek-Cypriot and we all were invited to his daughter's wedding which was a glorious affair spreading across many blocks of streets in Nicosia.

In contrast, our interactions with the Turks and Turkish-Cypriots were always more difficult and distant. Our meetings were formal and usually my discussions with Turkish-Cypriots were to tell them they could not do certain things. Watching a 1989 BBC documentary narrated by Christopher Hitchens reminded us of peacekeeping interactions with the Turks in Cyprus. In the documentary a Canadian captain, Bob Smallwood, is asking the Turks to not add sandbags to their portion of the demilitarized zone. I had told the Turkish officers the same thing nine years earlier. The Turkish army that manned the outposts on their side of the green line always viewed us suspiciously. They did not view us as an impartial and neutral force. Over time, I began to feel that the UN peacekeepers were really the Greek-Cypriot protection force. We were there to make sure that the Turks did not attack and take over the entire island given that they had been the aggressors only six years prior to our tour. I went back to Cyprus on a second peacekeeping tour in 1981 and found myself perplexed by the frustrating role of the UN. I believed then, and believe to this day, that the Turks would have taken the whole island if they had wanted to in 1974 or when I was there in 1980 and 1981. But they did not want the entire island, as that would have caused them enormous problems internationally and would have exacerbated an already serious refugee problem.

The invasion led to a massive refugee problem as Turkish-Cypriots in the south had to make their way north and even more Greek-Cypriots in the north were displaced from their homes and had to flee to the south. Some 200,000 Greek-Cypriots were forced to abandon their homes in the northern sector that was now controlled by Turkey. Taking only the northern part of the island meant that the Turks had somewhere to send the Greek-Cypriot refugees, which would not have been the case had they captured the entire island. More problematic for the Turks would have been the international reaction. Militarily the Turkish Army easily overwhelmed the Greek-Cypriots and their Greek protectors, who were no match for Turkey, which is ten times closer to Cyprus than is Greece.

The Turks advanced exactly to a line that had been discussed many times before—they went no further because they could make a plausible argument that they had taken by force what should have been theirs back in 1960 when partition of the island was seriously considered as the potential solution to the inter-communal conflict before independence was granted from Britain. The Turks were not held back by the UN in 1974 as they stopped where they wanted to stop and only then did the UN step in between the belligerent parties. If Turkey decided to take all of Cyprus today, both the Greek-Cypriots and the UN peacekeepers would be powerless to stop them. Certainly, the UN acted as a buffer between the two antagonists after the fact of the 1974 invasion and this prevented subsequent minor flare-ups, but I seriously questioned the need for the large UN presence by the time my tour ended in 1981. My views then may have been premature but I strongly believe that the time has come for the UN to move on. Today the UN is an obstacle to a solution.

The UN has been in Cyprus for fifty-eight years. Every single year the UN spends more than $50 million to keep UNFICYP (United Nations Peacekeeping Force in Cyprus) and more than 1,000 personnel in place. This is more personnel that the UN currently has between India and Pakistan and in Kosovo combined. There are many hot spots in the world that are much more in need of UN peacekeepers than an EU country such as Cyprus. A third of the UNFICYP expense is picked up by the Greek-Cypriot Government and a portion is paid by Greece but the UN still covers the bulk of the budget. That UNFICYP is partly funded by the Greeks and Greek-Cypriots makes clear which side wants the peacekeepers in place. UNFICYP has become the Greek-Cypriot protection force. With the UN as its protector, the Greek-Cypriots see no reason to compromise and thus the UN actually is a significant obstacle to a deal. Some 160 UN soldiers, including twenty-eight Canadian peacekeepers, have given their lives to bring peace to Cyprus. Every single UN Secretary-General going back to Dag Hammarskjold has invested considerable time and energy to bring peace to this 9,000-square-kilometer island with less than a million inhabitants. Every UN Secretary-General says this cannot go on forever, and yet it has.

The Cyprus problem, by and large, has faded from view given that the status quo seems acceptable to most parties. Most importantly, there has been no violence for close to twenty-five years, so why stir the hornet's nest? The current problem is that Cyprus is unresolved and the status quo is very much a sub-optimal outcome for both Greek and Turkish-Cypriots. Greek-Cypriots are being deprived of land and restitution and security, given the many Turkish troops on the island. The Turkish-Cypriots, despite having compromised to try to get a deal done with Greek-Cypriots, have been deprived of recognition which has made them outcasts in the international community. No country, other than Turkey, recognizes the Turkish-Cypriots and they cannot trade with the rest of the world nor can anyone fly directly to Turkish-Cyprus. The EU allowed a divided country to join it, which should have never happened, and the simmering dispute could easily lead to renewed conflict in this volatile region. We have seen intensified friction in the eastern Mediterranean between Turkey, Cyprus, Greece and even France. It is certainly not in the West's security interest to have two NATO powers come to blows. It is time for a solution. That means either both sides compromising and coming together as one nation or agreeing that the island should be permanently divided between a Greek-Cypriot nation and a Turkish-Cypriot one that can peacefully share the same island.

After my two peace-keeping tours, the Cyprus issue faded from my view for another twenty years until I went back to study at the Sorbonne in 2001-2002. I devoted my thesis to the role that the EU was playing at the time to help resolve the Cyprus problem. I wrote then that the EU had seriously misplayed its hand, particularly given that by 2002 it was clear that the EU was going to allow Cyprus into the EU, even without a solution, because that was the only way to get the greater EU enlargement done. The EU should never have started the accession process with Cyprus until the two Cypriot communities had resolved the situation on the island. It got involved in this mess because Greece forced the EU to admit Cyprus or else it would veto the larger eastern European enlargement, which was the EU's main objective. The EU initially gave the Turkish-Cypriots veto rights by telling the two sides of the island that they could not join unless they had found a solution to the division of the island. This led to the Turkish-Cypriots being completely unwilling to compromise or negotiate in good faith because they felt they held the trump card keeping Cyprus out of the EU. The EU then did a u-turn and decided that given this Turkish-Cypriot stonewalling they would allow Cyprus into the EU even if there was no solution. This became self-fulfilling, as now the shoe was on the other foot and the Greek-Cypriots were no longer willing to compromise since they saw a clear path to EU membership without having to give anything to the Turkish-Cypriots.

I believed then that allowing entry to a divided Cyprus would make any solution in the future even more difficult. The Greek-Cypriots would be allowed to join the EU, the island would remain divided, the Turkish-Cypriots would be forgotten and there would be no incentive for the Greek-Cypriots to compromise. Unfortunately, this is exactly what happened, and here we are some eighteen years later with no light at the end of the tunnel. The Greek-Cypriots thought that once they were in the EU, the Turkish-Cypriots would have no option but to capitulate, but this has not happened. The Greek-Cypriots thought their hand would be stronger but as time goes on their hand gets weaker and weaker as Turkey plays a more dominant role in the north of Cyprus.

As a Canadian, I have not been able to let go of Cyprus for two reasons. The first is that Canada was actually involved in Cyprus as peacekeepers starting in 1964 and Canadian peacekeepers stayed, and in many cases died, on the island for close to three decades. Canadians have, since the days of Lester Pearson, been known as great peacekeepers. As of 2019, some 125,000 Canadians have served in UN peace operations in many regions of the globe including Korea, India and Pakistan, Israel, Syria, Egypt, Namibia, Cambodia, Serbia, Croatia, Haiti, Rwanda, Kosovo, Bosnia and Herzegovina, Congo, and the Sudan, to name a few. When he served as minster of external affairs, Paul Martin Sr. was central to bringing UN forces to Cyprus back in 1964. Close to 35,000 Canadian soldiers have served in Cyprus over the years as peace-keepers. Brave Canadian peacekeepers stood tall and several were wounded in the 1974 Turkish invasion.

Both my first and last commanding officers in the army had played central roles in that fateful summer of 1974. My first com-manding officer when I joined 3 PPCLI in Victoria after college was Colonel Keith Corbould, who had commanded 2 Commando of the Canadian Airborne Regiment in Cyprus as a major in the summer of 1974. My last commanding officer when I served in the Special Service Force (SSF) was Brigadier-General Guy Lessard, who had commanded the Canadian Airborne Regiment in Cyprus in 1974. Both fine officers recounted the harrowing days in that turbulent summer as Canadian soldiers faced combat opera-tions for the first time since the Korean War. When I served in the Canadian army, probably the most common medal worn by troops was the blue and white Cyprus medal. Many soldiers served multiple peacekeeping missions in Cyprus, as did I. We fell in love with the island, its history, and the wonderful people on both sides of the green line. The Canadian connection continues to this day as the UN secretary-general's special representative for Cyprus is a Canadian diplomat, Ms. Elizabeth Spehar. I met with Ms. Spehar when I was in Nicosia in the summer of 2019, at the same camp where I served some forty years before. Ms. Spehar continues to seek a solution that will bring peace to the Cypriots.

The second reason that, as a Canadian, I can't let go of Cyprus is because the most obvious solution to the Cyprus political conundrum is a Canadian solution: confederation. Confederation is messy and confusing to many, including to Cypriots, as distinct levels of government are responsible for different areas of responsibility. As a senior Canadian diplomat who has closely covered the Cyprus file told us recently, "we Canadians know federalism. We accept that different levels of government can have different powers but Greek-Cypriots see this as very complicated."

Canada proves that confederation works. Canada is one of the most decentralized federations in the world as our central government even delegates some elements of foreign policy to a province to help protect minority rights. Decentralized power in a federation is especially important when there are "significant minorities" in the country. This is certainly the case in Canada and is the case in Cyprus. The Greek-Cypriots would prefer a unitary government where all the power lies with a central government that would of course be controlled by the majority, them. This option will never be the solution as it will never be accepted by the Turkish-Cypriots. If Cyprus is ever to be re-united, it will have to be in a confederation of two constituent parts, one Greek-Cypriot and one Turkish-Cypriot. Canada's example of shared power at the federal and provincial levels has led to several prominent Canadians being actively involved on the Cyprus file, including former Prime Minister Joe Clark and former Liberal Leader Stéphane Dion.

Canada is also an analogous example of ethnic tension. Canada's First Nations were joined by two other ethnic nationalities, English and French. From its earliest days, Canada's English and French communities have been divided by language, religion, culture, and history. One of my favourite novels exploring the French-English situation in Canada is Hugh MacLennan's *Two Solitudes*. The novel tells the story of the conflicts on both sides of the Tallard family in Quebec. It is an articulate exploration of the French-English divisions in Canada. Cyprus, in many ways, has that same ethnic divide and two solitudes of its own. The Greek-Cypriots and Turkish-Cypriots are similarly very different. They have religious, language, cultural, and historical differences. The Greek-Cypriots are descendants of the great Hellenic tradition and the Turkish-Cypriots are proud offspring of the Ottoman Empire.

But Canada has modeled how two nations can effectively cooperate as one to the benefit of both communities. Canada has been a functioning confederation for over 150 years. We share power at the provincial and federal levels of government. This always leads to tension but goodwill has kept Canada together. It has at times been a close call, but we have persevered and Canada is stronger as a result. Cyprus would be considerably stronger if it could reunite in a confederation of two nations under one common umbrella. There is no doubt that many important responsibilities would need to reside with each of the two constituent states in Cyprus. but over time, as both sides lived harmoniously together, one nation would be forged. The United States itself started life with power very much devolved to its own thirteen colonies. Compromises were made to form one nation that would go on to greatness despite many trials and tribulations along the way. Cyprus too can benefit by putting aside differences and finding common ground.

With a significant and vital French-Canadian minority, Canada also has had to be concerned about minority rights. French-Canadians are a majority in their own province of Quebec but they are a minority in Canada and certainly a small minority in anglophone North America as a whole. The Turkish-Cypriots are a majority in their isolated part of Cyprus but a minority in all of Cyprus. The Greek-Cypriots are a majority in Cyprus, but given that Turkey is only forty miles away they are a non-Muslim minority in the wider region. Both Northern Ireland and Israel/ Palestine have this same dilemma of a double minority to deal with. These situations are very troublesome to resolve but confederation is a workable solution as the Canadian experiment has so far proven. Canada is a richer country thanks to our ethnic and cultural diversity.

Symbols are also important when a nation has a significant minority, who may feel overwhelmed by the majority. Until the mid-1960s, Canada's flag featured the British Union Jack. This was hard for French-Canadians and First Nation Canadians to accept, and the new flag that was adopted could be embraced by English-Canadians, French-Canadians and First Nation Canadians. The fact that the Cypriot national anthem is also the Greek national anthem does not help bridge the ethnic divide in Cyprus. A re-united Cyprus will have to work to bridge these cultural, ethnic and religious divides. Compromise has made Canada possible. It has made for a richer and more vibrant country. The same would be true for Cyprus under a workable confederation. Reconciliation would make Cyprus a beacon of hope in a region that is torn by tribal conflicts.

Tribal conflicts are often difficult to solve, short of civil war. A couple of years ago I spent a week in Rwanda to understand how the genocide of 1994 could so quickly give way to relative peace and prosperity in that country. In that case, where so many lost their lives, peace came about because one side won. The Tutsi in Rwanda are greatly outnumbered by the Hutu majority. The Tutsi were the favourites of the colonial power, Belgium, but the Hutu took control after independence. The Tutsi were persecuted and many thousands slaughtered in the 1994 genocide. Today the Tutsi under President Kagame now hold all the levers of power having won the civil war against the Hutu after the 1994 genocide. Ruling with an iron fist, President Kagame has silenced all dissent. Not all parties are happy with the outcome but at the very least the genocide has stopped. The civil war in Rwanda ended some twenty years after the 1974 Turkish invasion of Cyprus and yet Rwanda is now on a path to reconciliation while the situation in Cyprus remains frozen. The good news is that there has been limited violence in Cyprus, but the bad news is that we are no closer to a solution today than we were forty years ago.

I have read many books, articles, and editorials on Cyprus, and so the obvious question must be, why another book on the same subject? Has it not all been said before? I think not. The shelves are full of brilliant analyses from both sides of the dispute and yet these millions of pages have not helped bridge the gap between these two communities. Almost all coverage is optimistic and hopeful, wishing for reconciliation and peace. But an enduring peace has been elusive for sixty years. False hope and unrealistic dreams do not a strategy make. Happy talk has gotten Cyprus nowhere.

Today in Cyprus, we find ourselves in the classic Nash equilibrium. Each side has a chosen strategy that they have pursued consistently since Cyprus entered the EU in 2004 and neither side sees a way to benefit by changing its strategy. Thus, we have static equilibrium, and the status quo is endurable, if not optimal, for both sides. That is why the status quo has lasted so long and why a catalyst is needed to change the situation.

The value of forty years of perspective is that I have become realistic in concluding that it is not possible to believe that the same approach will somehow lead to a different outcome for Cyprus. I do believe that we should try one more round of negotiations but I think it is time to tell both sides that this is the absolute last round of talks. Failure in the next round should be followed by an acceptance by both sides and by the international community at large that it is time to negotiate a "velvet divorce." This would lead to two separate recognized nations on the island; the Turkish-Cypriots would no longer be international outcasts. Such an outcome would actually be better for both communities than the current status quo as the north would be recognized and the Greek-Cypriots would get back land and restitution money, plus they would be secure in knowing that the security situation vis-à-vis Turkey had stabilized.

The bi-zonal bi-communal (BZBC) solution has been the default aim in all serious negotiations between the two sides. Bi-zonal essentially means that Cyprus would have two zones: one Greek-Cypriot and one Turkish-Cypriot. Bi-communal means that each community would be dominant and be protected to remain dominant in their zone or province or state. This would prevent, for example, Greek-Cypriots from buying up the Turkish-Cypriot properties in the Turkish-Cypriot zone and thus leading to the Turkish-Cypriot community being the minority in its own zone or province. The zone or province level would have jurisdiction over key community elements such as education and religion which would protect each ethnic group. The central government would include both communities with certain minority rights enshrined so that power was shared. It would also control items such as national security and foreign affairs. This BZBC solution is essentially confederation and remains the only possible means of reuniting the island into one nation. But after many hundreds of meetings, over many decades with BZBC as the default option, we are no closer to a solution. This book offers an alternative which is that both sides try to separate and live peacefully on the same island after a velvet divorce. It is worth one last try for a BZBC settlement to reunite the island, but my strong prediction is that time is running out and that the Greek-Cypriots, now safely home in the EU, will never make the compromises necessary to get Turkish-Cypriot and Turkish agreement for such a BZBC re-unification of the island.

Lord Hanney, who served as the UN special representative for Cyprus from 1996 to 2003, points out in his book that "the blame game was a specialty of the Greek-Cypriots. They played it day in and day out, and they played it well. If there had been an Olympic medal for playing the blame game, they would have won it. The Turks and Turkish-Cypriots played it very badly."[1] Undoubtedly, the Greek-Cypriots have built a better public-relations machine on the world stage, but I would tend to agree with former UK Foreign Minister Jack Straw, who told us that "both sides are incredibly good at the blame game." Finger pointing and talks have gone on for far too long. Cypriots do love to talk, as is illustrated by this old joke:

> Three men are sentenced to death in a faraway country: an Englishman, a Frenchman and a Cypriot. On the day of their execution, they are asked to name their last wish. The Englishman asks for a cigar; the Frenchman for a glass of wine. The Cypriot asks to be granted a last opportunity to talk to the execution squad about the Cyprus Problem. On hearing this, the Frenchman and Englishman change their last wish and beg to be shot before the Cypriot starts talking.

Surely, after fifty years, the time for talking is done as every issue has been hashed and rehashed hundreds of times. As one observer told us, this situation could be resolved over a weekend if both sides actually wanted to make a deal.

On my second tour peacekeeping in Cyprus, I went to see a terrific performance of Shakespeare's The Tempest in the open-air

---

1   David Hannay, Cyprus: *The Search for a Solution* (London: I.B. Tauris, 2005), 229.

theatre at the Curium, a Roman era theatre that was built starting in the second century BC. Sitting with fellow officers with our picnic baskets, watching lightning strike in the distance with the beautiful blue Mediterranean as the backdrop, was truly incredible. Appropriately, many see this play as an allegory of European colonization and side with Caliban who has lost his island to the exiled Prospero. Cyprus, like Caliban, has lost its beautiful island to outsiders for centuries. Cyprus has been the pawn for many empires dating back to Alexander the Great. Now is the time for the outside powers to allow the island to be its own truly independent nation or two nations if that turns out to be the democratic wish of Cypriots.

Why spend more effort now to challenge the status quo—a status quo that is in many ways livable for both sides? There are three reasons that a resolution would be significantly better than what we have now.

First, the continued division of the island has made the Turkish-Cypriots stateless for half a century. Since 2004, they have been willing to compromise to resolve the situation but they have not had a willing partner on the other side. This international isolation of the Turkish-Cypriots must end.

Second, Cyprus will continue to be a source of tension between Greece and Turkey, and Turkey and the EU, and Turkey and NATO, until the situation is resolved. That Cyprus serves as a flash point for conflict between NATO allies was seen recently when France sent Rafale fighters to the region to counter Turkish naval maneuvers aimed at frustrating gas exploration. This tiny spark cannot be allowed to start a major conflagration in what is already a volatile region of the world.

Finally, we would contend that a resolution would be better for both Cypriot communities. The Turkish-Cypriots would be recognized by the international community, but the main beneficiaries would be Greek-Cypriots. A solution would mean that they would no longer have a menacing foe across the green line, and they would have protection from Turkey, which is only forty miles away. They would benefit enormously economically, as there would be the recovery of lost land from both the Turkish-Cypriots and the British. They would also receive restitution for those properties they could not recover. Peace would also bring dramatically increased tourism to the island with its magnificent beaches, storied history, and cultural attractions. The absence of UN peacekeepers and a mutually acceptable resolution of the island's troubles would lead to an international influx of travelers who have never considered Cyprus as a tourist destination. A peaceful resolution would also allow for the economically efficient means of exploring, developing, and exporting the eastern Mediterranean gas near Cyprus, which would benefit all parties.

We are by nature meliorists and certainly believe that the world can be made better by human effort. Cyprus is certainly worth that effort. As authors, we take no sides in this long-standing dispute. For the last three years my daughter Glynnis, a historian, has been my co-researcher and co-author in this endeavor. Together we interviewed politicians, diplomats, and experts from both sides of this divide. We also spent a lot of time listening to objective non-Cypriots who, like us, only wish to help get to a solution for the island. We hope to provide the perspective of outside observers to encourage constructive dialogue which will lead to a break in a stalemate that has hurt all Cypriots. It is clear to us that the time for blaming the other side is over. It is time to make one last attempt to bridge the divide in a mutually acceptable BZBC con-federation, or agree to co-exist peacefully in two fully-sovereign nations. The United Nations should no longer be a prop for one side that is unwilling to move on after a fifty-year stalemate. Many other trouble zones could better use these precious resources.

PART ONE

The Road to Stalemate

"Those who do not remember the past are condemned to repeat it"

GEORGE SANTAYANA

CHAPTER 1

From Alexander to 1974

TODAY'S QUAGMIRE IN CYPRUS is the culmination of centuries of historical mistakes. The island is unfortunately a geographic crossroads, which leaves it ripe for conquest, and its past reads like a diary of intrusions by great powers.

Cyprus was colonized around the thirteenth century B.C. by settlers from the Aegean. Copper, which gave the island its name, was an important early export. Cypriot seafaring traders ranged as far as Syria, Egypt, Crete, and Sicily. Phoenicians settled on the island around the tenth century B.C., but over time Greek language and culture became dominant. At various stages, Cyprus was governed by the Greeks, the Phoenicians, the Assyrians, the Egyptians, and the Persians. The latter were particularly difficult to throw off the island, but when they were defeated by Alexander the Great, Cyprus was finally brought squarely into the Hellenic domain. Later on, Cyprus was part of the Roman Empire, and then an independent province under the Byzantine Empire.

After 395 AD., the entire island was Christianized. In 1191, during the Third Crusade, Richard the Lionheart conquered Cyprus. He sold the island in 1192 to the Knights Templar, which was ruled by a French noble family headed by Guy de Lusignan. Under the Lusignan dynasty, which lasted for three centuries, the island was arguably one of the world's richest countries, although its western-style feudal system rendered most of the inhabitants little more than serfs. The Latin Church was dominant, but the Greek Orthodox Church survived.

Venice and Genoa, two of the most prominent Italian city-states during the Renaissance era, fought over Cyprus to control its trade routes. In 1489, Cyprus was ultimately ceded to Venice, which used the island as a trading post and as a military base to defend against the Ottomans. As the Ottoman Empire expanded, many of the Venetian properties fell to this powerful foe and in 1571, Cyprus was taken by Sultan Selim II after bitter sieges of its major cities, Nicosia and Famagusta.

Many inhabitants welcomed the change from Venetian to Ottoman rule. The rights of the Greek Orthodox Church were returned with the Ottoman millet system. The millet was a separate court that allowed a religious community to rule itself under its own laws. Thus, the Greek Orthodox community became a largely self-governing religious group. The Ottomans brought about 20,000 Muslim colonists to the island but, now cut off from European trade routes, the once rich island experienced difficult economic times. Christians were forced to pay higher taxes, and a large number of residents converted to Islam.

Today, many optimists point to the Ottoman period as an example of the two communities living together, but this is a somewhat rosy reading of history. The two communities did cohabit but as Clement Dodd points out, they "lived in separate villages, or in separate parts of the same villages, mixing little and only rarely inter-marrying." Peace was generally maintained thanks to the power of the Ottoman Empire, but that was about to change.

When the Greeks finally decided to rise up against the Ottoman Empire in 1821, the European powers watched with great interest. Changing alliances and shifting boundaries in the Mediterranean can have a huge impact on the continent's political balance. The Ottoman Empire's strength had faded in the early nineteenth century, and many European countries feared Russia would drive into the Mediterranean and fill the power vacuum. Britain was particularly worried about any interruption of its trade routes to India.

Europe did not interfere in Cyprus right away. As the Greek rebellion continued during the 1820s, there were casualties on the island. The Greek Orthodox archbishop and many others were executed by Cypriot Ottoman rulers. But it was only in 1827, when the War of Independence seemed in peril, that Britain, France, and Russia joined forces on the side of the Greeks. The conflict was over by 1830, and 300 years of Ottoman rule in Cyprus ended.

Britain eventually took over the administration of Cyprus. The Greek-Cypriots had high expectations for British rule. Their success in the war had stirred up a nationalist Hellenism in the community, and the feeling was that liberal Britain would help them achieve *enosis*, a final union with Greece. They were disappointed. The British signed the Convention of Defensive Alliance with Turkey and stationed their fleet in Cyprus to secure the sea route to India via the Suez Canal, which was opened in 1869. And more unfortunately for the Cypriots, Britain got possession of Alexandria in 1882, which was more strategically located. It kept Cyprus as a pawn on its global chessboard but didn't invest in it. Britain thought so little of the island that it even entertained the Theodor Herzl notion of making Cyprus the national home for the Jews.

The British colonial administration operated through an eighteen-member legislative council (nine Greek-Cypriots, three Turkish-Cypriots, and six British). In 1914, when Turkey entered the Great War on Germany's side, Britain annexed Cyprus, and a year later promised the island to Greece if she would attack Bulgaria. Greece refused the offer. In 1923, Turkey recognized Britain's annexation of Cyprus with the signing of the Treaty of Lausanne. The combination of taxation and Greek-Cypriot demands for *enosis* led to a rebellion in 1931, during which the house of the British governor was burned. The rebels were eventually deported.

During World War II, some 25,000 Cypriots fought on the Allied side and this loyalty, combined with the worldwide wave of opposition to colonial rule, led to increased demands from the Greek-Cypriots in the 1950s. Britain maintained control of the island, as it did other colonies, although its divide-and-rule tactics left bitter scars. The occupier turned the Greeks and Turks against each other. C. M. Woodhouse, a British intelligence agent, claimed that "Harold Macmillan (then foreign secretary) was urging us to stir up the Turks in order to neutralize the Greek agitation."[2]

It wasn't difficult for the British to stir up conflict between Greeks and Turks on Cyprus, of course. The Greek-Cypriots were pushing for *enosis* while the Turkish-Cypriots, who made up 18 percent of the population, preferred *taksim*, or partition, with the British leaving. The Turk assumption that there would be *taksim* if the British left was not based on wishful thinking but on specific commitments made by the Brits. A statement in the House of Commons by Lennox Boyd, the British colonial secretary, outlined the case for partition:

> Any exercise of self-determination should be effected in such a manner that the Turkish-Cypriot community, no less than the Greek-Cypriot community shall, in the special circumstances of Cyprus, be given freedom to decide for themselves their future status—Her Majesty's Government recognizing that the exercise of self-determination in such a mixed population must include partition among the eventual options.[3]

Britain's control of Cyprus was increasingly tenuous as the twentieth century marched on, and the tensions came to a head in the mid-1950s. EOKA, The National Organization of Cypriot Fighters, began campaigning for independence, hoping ultimately

2 Christopher Hitchens, *Hostage to History* (New York: Verso, 1997), 43.
3 Clement Dodd, "New Perspectives," in *Cyprus The Need for New Perspectives*, ed. Clement Dodd (Cambridgeshire: Eothen Press,1999), 287-88.

to fulfill their dream of uniting with Greece. The Turkish community also wanted the British out, but it knew that this could compromise its own position. It remembered what had happened in Crete. Ottoman rule ended in Crete in 1896 after that island became independent with the help of Europe's great powers. Turkish Muslims made up one-ninth of Crete's population, but the European governments assured them that their independent status would be maintained and they wouldn't wake up one day to find themselves Greek. That's exactly what happened in 1913. Loath to see this same outcome repeated, Turkey demanded the return of the island if the British left Cyprus. Knowing that such a return of the island was unlikely, they were willing to settle for the second-best option: *taksim*. They got neither when Cyprus achieved independence in 1960.

The Zurich-London agreements of 1960, imposed by London, Athens, and Ankara, without input from the Cypriots, established the independent Republic of Cyprus, with Greek-Cypriot Archbishop Makarios as its first president (a significant symbolic mistake given the different religions of the two feuding communities). Virtually all parties were unhappy with the outcome, a compromise aimed at temporarily mollifying all parties rather than finding a long-term solution. The Brits wanted to end the fighting in Cyprus and leave the island. They also wanted to maintain their military presence on sovereign bases in Cyprus (they survive to this day). The Turkish-Cypriots feared EOKA and the Greek-Cypriots were furious at what they viewed as Britain's betrayal in the compromises they were forced to make with respect to Turkish-Cypriot governance rights, which fell well short of *enosis*.

The Turkish-Cypriots, now ruled by a Greek-Cypriot archbishop, were miles from *taksim*. As Niels Kadritzke observed: "The 1960 republic of two communities could only be a dilatory compromise for the Greek and Turkish elites, standing in the way of their respective maximalist positions: *enosis* (union with Greece) and *taksim* (division)."[4] The Cypriots were "simply presented with the results and told brusquely that if they did not accept them, they would be faced with partition."[5]

Like many other geopolitical solutions imposed by Britain (India/Pakistan and Palestine, to name but two), this compromise was fatally flawed. As Felipe Fernandez-Armesto points out in *Millenium*: "The curse of de-colonization was the creation of states without history, extemporized for convenience, bereft of traditional elites or colonial peace-keepers, partitioned previously or federated whimsically."[6]

Turkey agreed to independence for Cyprus only if the Turkish-Cypriots were guaranteed equal partnership rights in government. In fact, as Glen Camp has said: "Their insistence on specific, rigid provisions expressed their (Turkish-Cypriot) misgivings about their fate as a minority."[7] To ensure that they were protected, the basic articles of the constitution were declared to be unalterable.

---

4   Niels Kadritzke, "From Missile Crisis to EU Membership," *Le Monde Diplomatique*, August-September 1998, 1.
5   Nicholas Pope, "Le durcissement turc sur la question chypriote risqué de devenir un case-tete pour les Quinze," *Le Monde*, June 1,2001, 49.
6   Felipe Fernandez-Armesto, *Millenium* (Toronto: Doubleday, 1995), 533.
7   Glen Camp, "Greek-Turkish Conflict over Cyprus," *Political Science Quarterly* 95, no. 1 (Spring 1980): 49.

For further protection, Article 4 of the 1960 Treaty of Guarantee provided a role for Turkey in the event that Turkish-Cypriots rights were altered. It stated that Turkey reserved the right "to take action with the sole aim of re-establishing the state of affairs created by the present treaty."[8] This right of intervention, shared by the three guaranteeing powers (Britain, Greece, and Turkey), would prove critical in 1974.

The compromise of 1960 immediately proved unworkable. As Glen Camp notes:

> Without some minimal consensus between the two communities, the ponderous and ramshackle structure of the Zurich-London accords was almost sure to collapse. It is hard to accept the accords as anything but a desperate and really unworkable compromise dictated by grim political exigency. The accords were in effect to substitute legal structure for political consensus.[9]

As one respected Turkish-Cypriot cabinet minister noted: "Whilst the Turkish-Cypriot partner regarded the 1960 compromise as an end in itself, the Greek-Cypriot partner merely regarded it as a means to an end, namely, as a means of achieving its ultimate objective of *enosis*."[10]

---

8   Hitchens, *Hostage to History*, 97-98.
9   Camp, "Greek-Turkish Conflict," 46.
10 Necati Munir Ertekun, "the Turkish Cypriot Outlook," in *Cyprus The Need for New Perpspectives*, ed. Clement Dodd (cambridgeshire: Eothen Press, 1999), 98.

Greek-Cypriots, in their defense, would claim that the 1960 treaties were "colonial" accords that had been forced on them. The agreement was obviously a compromise, given their clearly articulated and oft-repeated demand to unite with Greece. Greek-Cypriots viewed the Turkish-Cypriots as a minority who should have a say equivalent to their proportion of the population (18 percent at that time) rather than as an equal political partner. The inalterability of the basic elements of the constitution and a Turkish-Cypriot veto on most major decisions was not what the Greek-Cypriots viewed as a long-term solution. For any chance of success, the 1960 accords required empathy, compromise, and a fine sense of fairness between the two communities. This was clearly not the situation.

The experiment of living peacefully together without an outside master lasted only three years. In 1963, Makarios started to undermine the rights Turkish-Cypriots by curbing the power of their municipalities. These rights had been an essential element of the 1960 constitution. On April 27, 1963 the constitutional court issued a ruling declaring that this curtailing of Turkish-Cypriot power was invalid but "Makarios had already publicly declared in February that he would not comply with the decisions of the Court in respect of Turkish municipalities."[11]

Makarios went to Ankara to meet with Turkish Prime Minister Inonu. He promised he had no intention of changing the Cypriot constitution and, should questions arise, he would consult with

11   Salahi Sonyel, "New Light on the Genesis of the Conflict," in *Cyprus The Need for New Perspectives*, 25.

the Turkish government.[12] He did not keep his word, and threw out the constitution on November 30, 1963, proclaiming his own doctrine which significantly curtailed the power of the Turkish-Cypriot minority.

Makarios had devised a plan (The Akritas Plan) for a campaign of violence against the Turkish-Cypriots to "oblige them to comply with Greek-Cypriot demands for constitutional change."[13] It was initiated on December 21, 1963. The Turkish-Cypriots would be effectively ghettoized into "secure" enclaves.

The British immediately understood the severity of Makarios' plan. As N.J.A. Cheetham of the foreign office noted in a memo: "The Turks undoubtedly have a strong legal case. They are also probably right in thinking that Makarios' general purpose is to whittle away the constitutional rights of the Turkish community."[14]

George Ball of the U.S. State Department reported that the Greek-Cypriots were undertaking a systematic genocide of the Turkish-Cypriot population. As he told Washington, "Their only desire is to liquidate the Turkish population."[15]

Ernest Forsthoff, the former president of the Supreme Constitutional Court of Cyprus, told a journalist on December 30, 1963: "All this happened because Makarios wanted to remove all constitutional rights from the Turkish-Cypriots. From the

12   Sonyel, "New Light," 22.
13   Clement Dodd, "a Historical Overview," in *Cyprus The Need for New Perspectives*, 7.
14   Sonyel, "New Light," 24.
15   Sonyel, "New Light," 32.

moment Makarios started openly to deprive the Turkish-Cypriots of their rights, the present events were inevitable."[16]

The Greek-Cypriot inspired violence resulted in nearly 30,000 Turkish-Cypriots being relocated from 103 mixed villages. After their departure, their homes were burned by their Greek-Cypriot neighbours. Turkish-Cypriot enclaves were blockaded, and many who ventured out were abducted and never seen again. Professor Salahi Sonyel reports that "bodies were later found in bulldozed mass graves."[17] The only time the Turkish-Cypriot politician Rauf Denktaş became visibly emotional and agitated in my ninety-minute interview with him in Nicosia in 2002 was when he recalled the events of 1963-64:

> They thought they could just get rid of us all in two or three days. On 21 December 1963, they started the attacks. One doctor in Larnaca who had Turkish-Cypriots as 80 percent of his patients donned his captain's uniform and attacked his patients. Makarios had all his cabinet with their own secret militias. What the Greek-Cypriots did was state-sponsored terrorism. They lined up 20 or 25 school children and shot them.

With the Turkish-Cypriots in a state of siege, the Turkish Air Force flew sorties over Nicosia on Christmas Day, 1963. On January 12, 1964 the British High Commission in Nicosia wrote to London that, "The Greek (Cypriot) police are led by extremists who provoked

16   Sonyel, "new Light," 29.
17   Sonyel, "New Light," 31.

the fighting and deliberately engaged in atrocities." Makarios had given assurances that there would be no attacks, and his assurances, it was now decided, were "as worthless as previous assurances have proved."[18]

The Greek-Cypriot assault continued. The Turkish-Cypriot quarter of Limassol was attacked with tanks on February 13, 1964. When the final toll was counted, more than 300 Turkish-Cypriots had disappeared without a trace during the events of 1963-64.

A sort of truce was established in June 1964 when Ankara, declaring the situation of the Turkish-Cypriots intolerable, threatened invasion. It was dissuaded from this course by Washington. UN Forces were sent to the island, essentially to protect the Turkish-Cypriot minority.

Interestingly, the preferred policy prescription of the outside power, this time the United States, was similar to the option considered by Britain as Cyprus lurched towards independence in the late 1950s: partition. George Ball told a British officer who claimed that a unitary state was possible, "You've got it wrong, son. There's only one solution to this island and that's partition."[19]

Trouble returned to Cyprus in 1967, again precipitated by Makarios. He sent police patrols into two Turkish-Cypriot villages, Ayias Theodora and Kohphinou, at a "cost of over thirty Turkish-Cypriot lives." Ankara again threatened to attack and again the United States intervened to prevent a conflict between two NATO

---

18   Michael Stephen, "How the International Community made a Cyprus Settlement Impossible," *Perceptions* 6, no. 1 (March- May 2001):4.
19   Hitchens, *Hostage to History*, 5.

members. President Johnson sent a special envoy, Cyrus Vance, to settle things down, and a relative calm prevailed from 1967 until 1974, but in no way was that status quo acceptable to the Turkish-Cypriots. Effectively, Greek-Cypriots were in control of the island's government and most of its terrain, and things were about to get much worse.

Any balanced reading of Cypriot history prior to 1974 shines a bright light on the systematic marginalization and brutalization of the Turkish-Cypriot minority. Unfortunately, few EU diplomats bother with Cypriot history prior to 1974. Current Greek-Cypriot revisionists like to portray the sordid episodes the 1960s as aberrations of fringe fanatics; they paint a flattering portrait of Makarios as an innocent bystander, never mind that a UK House of Commons select committee wrote in 1986-87 that most of the violence "was either directly inspired by, or certainly connived at, by the Greek-Cypriot leadership."[20] British high commissioner Lyn Parker was blunter with us in Cyprus in 2002: "There is no doubt that in the 1960s, the Greek-Cypriots perpetrated horrible things against the Turkish-Cypriots."

One need only take Makarios' own words to understand that compromise was not in his nature. In a September 4, 1962 speech in his native village of Panayia, Makarios said, "unless this small Turkish community, forming a part of the Turkish race, which has been the terrible enemy of Hellenism, is expelled, the duty of the heroes of EOKA can never be considered as terminated."[21]

---

20   Stephen, "How the International Community," 5.
21   Sonyel, "New Light," 20-21.

Glen Camp rightly claims that had Makarios "chosen to press for renegotiation instead of indulging in a willful act of unilateral abrogation, the tragedy . . . might have been avoided."[22]

---

22 Camp, "Greek -Turkish Conflict," 50.

CHAPTER 2

The Crisis of 1974

GREECE WAS RULED BY A military junta known as the Regime of the Colonels from 1967 to 1974. At the end of this period, the junta's leader, Brigadier Ioannides, decided to solve the Cyprus problem unilaterally. Talks with Turkey had gone nowhere, and the junta wanted rid of Markarios, whom it believed was not sufficiently aggressive.

On July 3, 1974 Makarios triggered his own demise by writing an open letter to General Gizikis, the puppet president of Ioannides' regime, complaining about the junta. He claimed that the Greek military was directing the activities of a Greek-Cypriot terrorist organization known as EOKA B. "I have more than once so far, felt, and in some cases, I have touched, a hand invisibly extending from Athens and seeking to liquidate my human existence," said Markarios.[23] Twelve days later he was overthrown by

---

23 Hitchens, *Hostage to History*, 81.

the junta. It bombed his palace, planning to kill the archbishop, but he escaped. EOKA B snipers killed the U.S. Ambassador and installed a violent ex-EOKA leader, Nicos Sampson, known as "the Turk killer," as president of Cyprus.

The plan was to unite Cyprus with Greece, at last achieving the *enosis* which had long been the dream of Greek-Cypriot national-ists, but the coup was condemned around the world. The *New York Times* reported on July 19, 1974, "It is almost beyond belief that the Greek officers would attempt to install as President of Cyprus one Nikos Sampson, confessed murderer, professional bully boy and fanatical supporter of *enosis.*"

Three days after the Sampson coup, Turkish Prime Minister Bulent Ecevit, who had been a pupil of Kissinger's at Harvard, flew to London to convince the UK to enforce the 1959 Treaty of Guarantee. He quickly learned that the British were not prepared to meet their obligations. It wasn't Turkey's first disappointment. Turkish-Cypriots had called on Britain to protect them from geno-cide under Article 4 of the Cyprus treaty in 1963, 1967 and 1974, and three times they were refused.

The Turks had threatened invasion in 1963 and 1967 but held back, in no small part because of US pressure. Now facing an unambiguous final solution at the hands of the Greeks, and with President Nixon's administration preoccupied with the last act of Watergate, Turkey had a clear path and the unilateral right to respond to the junta-inspired breakdown of Cyprus' constitu-tional order. On July 20, 1974, Turkish forces invaded Cyprus—a "legal intervention," in Turkish terminology. As Nanette Neuwahl argued in a Harvard Jean Monnet Working Paper, "International law endows Turkey with a role in the region and entitles it to exercise its influence there."[24]

The Turkish invasion on July 20, codenamed Operation Atilla, started with a dawn landing of some 3,000 troops and twelve tanks on the north coast of Cyrpus, just to the west of Kyrenia. A ceasefire was hastily negotiated three days later, but it would not hold. On August 14, the second phase of the invasion was launched: a larger force of 40,000 Turkish troops and some 180 tanks. Paratroopers were dropped and numerous air sorties were flown from Turkey. The Turkish army quickly achieved its objectives and controlled the northern part of the island.

The strategic importance of Cyprus was obvious to Turkey's leaders. In addition to their duty to protect Turkish-Cypriots, they couldn't abide their archenemy's domination of an island forty miles from their shores. Cyprus had become a dagger pointed directly at Turkey. As Turan Gunes, Turkey's Foreign Minister, said:

> Cyprus is as precious as the right arm of a country which cares for her defence or her expansionistic aims if she harbours any. If we don't keep this strategic importance of Cyprus we cannot understand the peace operation of 20 July [1974] or rather it is impossible to understand the entire Cyprus crisis . . . Many states, to a certain extent because it suits their interest, want to see the Cyprus problem merely as our desire to protect the Turkish community on the island. Whereas, the actual problem

24   Nanette Neuwahl, " Cyrprus Which Way? In Pursuit of a Confederal Solution in Europe," *Harvard Law School Jean Monnet Working Pape*r (April 2000): 15.

is the security of 45 million Turks in the motherland together
with the Turks in the island and the maintenance of the balance in the Middle East.[25]

With the US on the sidelines, and his own military likely to oust
him if he did not act, Ecevit had little choice but to answer Greece's
obvious provocation with an invasion. His naval commander,
Admiral Karacan, told him frankly, "Mr. Prime Minister, if we turn
back from Cyprus, I won't be able to remain naval commander-in-
chief and you won't be able to remain prime minister."[26]

Most legal scholars claim that this first invasion was legal
under international law, given Turkey's rights under the Treaty
of Guarantee. After this first invasion, the Turks presented proposals in Geneva to solve the crisis. These proposals effectively
offered a version of a bi-zonal, bi-communal arrangement. This
fact is seldom mentioned by Greek-Cypriots. It is true that the
Turks were negotiating from a position of strength at the time
and that its offer was effectively an ultimatum, but it does show
that Turkey was willing to minimize its intervention if it could
come to an acceptable solution for Cyprus. With no resolution
forthcoming from Geneva, Turkey launched phase two of the invasion between August 14-16 and effectively divided Cyprus in two,
with the Turkish-Cypriots controlling the north 37 percent of the

---

25   Alper Kaliber, "re-imagining Cyprus: the rise of regionalism in Turkey's security
      lexicon," in *Cyprus a conflict at a Crossroads*, eds. Thomas Diez and Nathalie Tocci
      (Manchester: Manchester University Press, 2013), 114.
26   Hitchens, *Hostage to History*, 96.

island. Interestingly, the Turkish Army halted its advance exactly on the line proposed by Turkey as the demarcation for partition in 1965, which was rejected at the time by the United Nations. Turkish-Cypriots in the south headed north, and some 180,000 Greek-Cypriot refugees headed South.

Legal opinion splits on the legality of this second stage of the invasion. Each side trots out its own scholars to argue its case. It is clearly ambiguous, but the international community has generally viewed this second move as illegal. If the Turks had somehow combined the two phases of their attack into one and divided the island in one fell swoop, these same analysts would have viewed the Turkish intervention as legal. But because three weeks separated the two moves, the second move was deemed illegal. This is legal hair-splitting. The reason that the invasion was split into two phases was that Turkey hoped to get a negotiated settlement in Geneva. Whether or not one agrees with Turkey's move, one thing is clear: for the Turkish-Cypriots, Turkey solved the lingering Cyprus problem. Nicos Sampson told a Greek newspaper in 1981 that "had Turkey not intervened in 1974, I would not only have proclaimed *enosis*—I would have annihilated the Turks in Cyprus."[27]

Turkey, then, did not provoke this crisis. It acted in self defense. It was provoked in 1963 and 1967 and showed restraint, even though it had the legal right to intervene in both cases. After those incidents, it developed contingency plans to deal with any future crises, and the Greek coup in 1974 was clearly such a crisis.

27   Stephen, "How the International Community," 2.

Given that both Greece and Turkey were NATO members and large beneficiaries of US financing, the US alone had the leverage on both parties to bring about a settlement and to contain the conflict. In the 1960s, US policy had been designed to maintain relations with both Greece and Turkey as NATO allies. As Monteagle Stearns, former US ambassador to Greece, stated:

> We simply tried to fit Greece and Turkey into our Soviet policy and the fit was never a comfortable one . . . It meant we discounted the importance of regional problems – the problem of Cyprus, the problem of the Aegean, and the problem of Greek-Turkish relations generally because we believed, incorrectly, that when Greece and Turkey were admitted into NATO in 1952, their ultimate security aspirations had been achieved. Everything else was of lesser concern. And this was, of course, far from the truth.[28]

The US in the 1960s was also concerned that, as Christopher Hitchens notes, "Cyprus might become the Cuba of the Mediterranean with Makarios as its cassocked Castro."[29] As the *New York Times* reported on August 1, 1961, "There is only one country where [the Soviet Union] may reasonably hope to see communism take over by normal democratic procedure. That country is Cyprus." This fear of communism's expansion into the Eastern Mediterranean drove US Cypriot policy during the

---

28 Monteagle Stearns, *Entangled Allies: US Policy toward Greece, Turkey and Cyprus* (New York: Council on Foreign Relations Press, 1992),13.
29 Hitchens, *Hostage to History*, 57.

Lyndon Johnson years. In 1964, that fear drove the US Ambassador in Nicosia, Fraser Wilkins, to tell Makarios: "If unrest develops in this island and the Turkish government decides to intervene, the US Government will take the line that they are perfectly within their rights under the Treaty of Guarantee."[30]

The US did not follow through on that 1964 threat. Ultimately, it did the opposite and specifically prevented the Turkish Government from intervening. LBJ sent the Turkish prime minister a June letter warning that the US would not use NATO to prevent a Soviet attack on Turkey if the Soviets reacted to a Turkish invasion of Cyprus. This stopped any Turkish invasion plans, but it also cooled relations between the US and Turkey. The Turks were flabbergasted by the letter and in 1965 requested that the US stop using Turkish bases for reconnaissance flights over Soviet territory.

After the US intervened to prevent Turkey from invading Cyprus during the 1967 crisis, Turkish leaders, feeling betrayed, began to expand relations with the Soviet Union. The intention was to gain more power within the Western alliance by flirting with a competing superpower. The Soviets were happy to oblige the Turks, who by the 1970s became one of the larger beneficiaries of Soviet aid outside the Warsaw Pact. This Turkish overture towards the Soviet Union must be kept in mind when one considers the US role in the 1974 Cyprus crisis.

Cynics like Christopher Hitchens argued that the US wanted the invasion to happen, believing that it would solve the Cyprus

---

30 Sonyel, "New Light," 32.

problem and settle the animosity between the two NATO members, once and for all. In his excellent *Hostage to History*, Hitchens claims that Ball, representing the US, was aware of the Greek plot to overthrow Makarios and that "by helping further to poison an ethnic conflict, the United States deliberately created the very conditions which it was later to cite, hypocritically, as the justification for partition."[31]

Given US intelligence capabilities it is certainly plausible that the US had advance knowledge of the Greek junta's plans but Hitchens' criticism is unfair, assuming as it does that the US was somehow able to predict how these events would play out. The US has proven repeatedly over the decades that it is not capable of playing a sophisticated and long-term game in international relations, as we have witnessed in both Afghanistan and more ominously in Iraq. The real reasons are rather different from Hitchens' suppositions.

The first is that the US almost certainly believed that the invasion would turn out differently. Ex-State Department official and Bryant University professor Glen Camp points out "Washington followed a single, pre-meditated unswerving pro-Turkish partition policy from the Acheson-Ball Plan of 1964 to Kissinger's tilt towards Ankara of 1974."[32] The US believed the end result would be a divided island which would be accepted by all sides (albeit with much less territory for the Turkish forces) and thus a thorny problem would be solved and peace would be maintained in NATO.

31   Hitchens, *Hostage to History*, 160.
32   Camp, "Greek-Turkish Conflict," 53.

The second reason that the US did not prevent the 1974 invasion is because the US continued to dislike Makarios and his foreign policy positions. Makarios was anti-American and during the Cold War had few friends in Washington. Any solution that removed Makarios was certain to be acceptable to Washington.

The third reason that the US gave Turkey more latitude to act was to prevent its leaders from shifting their position more towards the Soviet Union, which had become a serious US concern.

The fourth and final reason the US stood aside was Watergate. In the summer of 1974, the US national security team was worried that its major foe, the Soviet Union, would take advantage of the turmoil in Washington. As Timothy Naftali writes in *The Wounded Presidency*:

> With the Nixon presidency in its death throes, Kissinger still worried about the Soviets making trouble. But the only countries that actually attempted to exploit the widening power vacuum in Washington during this period were the small ones. In mid-July, Greece had overthrown the government of Cyprus, prompting Turkey to invade the Mediterranean island . . . Nixon and Kissinger had previously discussed what to do if Greece retaliated by attacking Turkey in Thrace. Despite the weakened State of Nixon's presidency, the Department of Defense and the CIA suggested covert action to overthrow the Greek regime.[33]

33 Timothy Naftali, "The Wounded Presidency, Part One," Foreign Affairs, January 28, 2020

Kissinger objected to this plan and the US did not need to intervene. The Greek government fell without a US push.

The Turks and the Turkish-Cypriots, victims of the July 1974 coup, reacted forcefully and decisively to resolve the Cyprus "problem." In the forty-five years since, there have been fewer Cypriot deaths than there were in single days pre-1974. The international community which chastises Turkey for its actions has been staggeringly hypocritical. Turkey's intervention in Cyprus certainly stands on more solid legal grounds than the US invasions of Grenada, Panama, or Iraq. The British have no right to castigate Turkey when they maintain bases in Cyprus, solely as an extension of imperial power. Is it somehow legal for the Brits to extend themselves deep into the Mediterranean but not for the Turks to protect their own backyard? Unfortunately for Turkey, the international community still holds that its 1974 action was illegal, one of the few consistent notes in its approach to Cyprus.

In fairness to the international community, any reading of the Treaty of Guarantee makes clear that Turkey must return Cyprus to what it was in the 1960 constitution. This means that Turkey is bound to try to resolve the conflict and create one state. It cannot argue that the treaty authorized its intervention and then disregard the same treaty's prohibitions against partitioning Cyprus. The legal requirement is to negotiate to recapture the spirit and intention of the 1960 constitution, which was a bi-communal agreement. However, having been burned consistently between 1963 and 1974, it is fair for the Turks to demand something a bit more substantial and re-assuring in order to protect the Turkish-Cypriot minority.

The Greek-Cypriots only cared about these constitutional niceties after 1974. They switched from being aggressors to the aggrieved party. The Greek junta's takeover of Cyprus had put Greek-Cypriots in the worst possible position. An action that had been designed to achieve the maximalist objective, *enosis*, ironically triggered the Turkish invasion, and in practical terms achieved the Turkish-Cypriot maximalist objective of partition of the island, *taksim*. The Greek junta can be credited with one of the most self-defeating moves of any military junta in the twentieth century, only to be outdone in 1982 by the Argentine junta that attacked the Falkland Islands and Saddam Hussein's 1990 invasion of Kuwait.

During the many post-1974 attempts to resolve the impasse in Cyprus, the Turkish-Cypriots have been portrayed in the international press as inflexible. This has sometimes been the case but, again, it is a partial view of the picture. On several occasions since 1974, the Greek-Cypriot side has stymied negotiations. The UN Secretary General came close to a resolution in 1985-86 when agreements were accepted by Turkish-Cypriots but effectively rejected by their Greek-Cypriot counterparts. The *Times* reported in June 1986 that "The UN Secretary-General has cast his usual diplomatic discretion aside to blame the Greek-Cypriot community for obstructing his attempts at a negotiated settlement to the Cyprus dispute."

Similarly, the Greek-Cypriots caused the breakdown of another UN effort led by Dr. Boutros Boutros-Ghalis' in 1992. Said Rauf Denktaş in 2002:

When we met in New York to discuss the Set of Ideas in 1992, I was told beforehand that Vassiliou had accepted all 100 points and that I should compromise on the 8 points which I still wanted to discuss. But when Vassiliou came to the meeting he said that he had not agreed to any of the 100 points and we had to discuss them all. What had really happened was that it was the election time and he was campaigning against Clerides who was claiming that the Set of Ideas was a sell-out to the Turks.

This Turkish-Cypriot version of the rejection of the 1992 Set of Ideas meets with the agreement of a number of independent observers including Zenon Stavrinides, the UN General Secretary for the Association for Cypriot Greek and Turkish Affairs. Clerides used his criticism of the Set of Ideas to secure his win in the presidential elections of February 1993. Thus Greek-Cypriot political expediency undermined a viable peace process in 1992. The UN Secretary General also tried to put in place some confidence-building measures in early 1993, which the Turkish-Cypriot side accepted; these were also rejected by the Greek-Cypriots.

Suffice to say, both sides have been responsible at various times for the failure to reach an acceptable solution since 1974. Given the number of interested parties and domestic politics in Greece, Turkey, and Cyprus, it has generally been difficult, if not impossible, to line up all the moons to secure a deal.

CHAPTER 3

The UN: Paved With Good Intentions

"THE UNITED NATIONS," said its second secretary general, Dag Hammarskjold, "was not created in order to bring us heaven, but in order to save us from hell." His organization has been involved in Cyprus for more than a half century now, and its efforts to find a solution to the island's problems have been continuous and extensive. Napoleon dismissed the Pope by asking famously, "how many divisions does the Pope have?" The UN is similarly constrained, as it has no divisions and thus cannot be a peacemaker but must be content to be a peacekeeper. Some 180 UN soldiers from many nations, including twenty-six Canadians, have died keeping the peace in Cyprus, and the UN's headquarters in Nicosia has a Wall of Honour in their memory. They can rest assured that they achieved Hammarskjold's limited objective of saving the island from hell. Unfortunately, the UN's usefulness on the island is now at an end, with the two sides being further apart than they were back in the early days of peacekeeping.

The original UN peacekeeping force in Cyprus, UNFICYP, was established in March 1964. It was hurriedly assembled after the breakdown of constitutional order in Cyprus led to fighting in the last weeks of 1963. UN Security Council Resolution 186 declared that UNFICYP's mandate was to preserve "international peace and security, to use its best efforts to prevent a recurrence of fighting and, as necessary, to contribute to the maintenance and restoration of law and order and a return to normal conditions." Composed of soldiers from the UK, Austria, Canada, Finland, Sweden, and Ireland, UNFICYP was supposed to stay on the island for three months.

The presence of UN troops certainly helped calm the situation and prevented large-scale fighting, but Cypriots do not recall this period with fondness. Turkish-Cypriots believed the UN presence was intended not so much to keep the peace as to protect the Greeks. Greek-Cypriots were equally displeased. As US Under Secretary of State George Ball said, "The Greek-Cypriots do not want a peace-keeping force; they want to be left alone to kill Turkish-Cypriots."

The UN appointed former Ecuadorian president Galo Plaza Lasso as its mediator in Cyprus. He published a sixty-page report in March 1965 that was critical of both sides. Galo Plaza Lasso came out against the Greek-Cypriots' preferred *enosis* solution. This might have seemed to favour Turkey and the Turkish-Cypriots but, as Christopher Hitchens noted, the report rejected the idea of partition and supported an independent unitary state (as opposed to a federation). The Turkish-Cypriots opposed this direction and rejected the whole of the Galo Plaza Lasso report on grounds that he had overstepped his mandate, which had been to act as a mediator rather than to submit formal proposals.

The UN role after the Galo Plaza Lasso report was rather muted, despite some intercommunal talks in the period 1968 to 1974. These made little progress and were halted by the Turkish invasion of 1974.

In April 1975, UN Secretary General Kurt Waldheim launched a new round of discussions. These led to a substantial breakthrough on February 12, 1977, when the two leaders, Rauf Denktaş and Archbishop Makarios, signed a four-point agreement which confirmed that any future solution would be based on a federation of two states (bi-zonal) and two communities (bi-communal). This agreement marked a significant concession by the Greek-Cypriots as they now accepted that the Turkish-Cypriots would in effect control their own zone and that the Greek-Cypriot dream of *enosis* was dead. Nevertheless, the two sides were still miles apart on the specifics of the plan and the talks eventually collapsed.

A year later, the US, UK, and Canada outlined a twelve-point plan that was presented to both sides by the UN secretary general. Much like the 1977 plan, this one called for a federation of two states. The central government would handle foreign affairs, external defense, banking, foreign trade, customs, immigration, and civil aviation. Any issue not specifically assigned to the central government would be the responsibility of the two states. The proposal also envisaged a reduction of foreign troops and power sharing in the central government. Despite this plan being broadly in line with the 1977 proposal, the Greek-Cypriots rejected it because it did not guarantee freedom of settlement, freedom of movement, and the right of return of property.

In May 1979, Secretary General Waldheim visited Cyprus and agreed on a ten-point set of proposals with the two sides. These talks covered issues such as the potential opening of Nicosia International Airport and what to do about Varosha, the famed tourist quarter of the port city of Famagusta, which has been abandoned in 1974. This round floundered on "bi-zonality." The Turkish-Cypriots wanted a true confederation of equals, whereas the Greek-Cypriots wanted a federal system where sovereignty lies with the central state.

The UN efforts suffered a severe setback in 1983 when the Turkish Cypriots unilaterally declared independence and formed the "Turkish Republic of Northern Cyprus" (TRNC). The UN condemned the move but continued to seek a solution. Under the new UN Secretary-General, Javier Perez de Cuellar, the peace process was resumed early in 1984. After several rounds of negotiations, the two sides met in January 1985 for their first face-to-face talk since 1979. The intent was to finalize an agreement; unfortunately, Greek-Cypriot leader Achilleos Kyprianou seized the opportunity to continue negotiations, which led to the talks collapsing once again. This was a win for Denktaş and a PR disaster for Kyprianou.

It was the same story that everyone had seen many times over: whether a four-point, ten-point, or twelve-point plan, one side (in the latter case, the Turkish-Cypriots) would be willing to make concessions while the other side could not bring itself to a final settlement.

The UN and Javier Perez de Cuellar did not give up. In March 1986, de Cuellar presented a draft framework agreement to both parties. Again, the basis was a bi-communal, bi-zonal federal state. Greek-Cypriots had a long list of problems this time around: they objected to the continued presence of Turkish troops on the island; to the proposal's failure to address repatriation of Turkish settlers to Turkey; to its insufficiently centralized federal structure; and to the absences of guarantees for freedom of settlement, freedom of movement, and the right of return of property. The draft was shelved and talks resumed in August 1988 with George Vassiliou as the new Greek-Cypriot leader.

The UN presented a new Set of Ideas to the two parties in June 1989. This time it was the Turkish-Cypriots who summarily rejected the proposal. Denktaş made the same arguments that the Turkish-Cypriots had made with respect to the Galo Plaza Report back in 1965: the UN had no right to present formal plans but could only serve as the mediator. The talks ended abruptly when Cyprus formally applied to join the European Community in July 1990. Denktaş was furious. Javier Perez de Cuellar blamed the failure on Turkish-Cypriot demands for equal sovereignty and for the right to secede. This was a missed opportunity for Cyprus as most observers gave Vassiliou credit for his willingness to compromise.

In January 1992 Boutros Boutros-Ghali became UN Secretary General and like all of his predecessors, he was optimistic that he could square the Cyprus circle. Ghali and the UN team proposed yet another Set of Ideas based on a bi-zonal, bi-command federation that would have prohibited any form of secession (a key Greek-Cypriot demand) or union with another state (whether Greece or Turkey). The Greek-Cypriots accepted this basis. Denktaş, again, was the reluctant party. The Turkish-Cypriot leader accepted 91 of the 100 proposals in Ghali's plan but he was completely unwilling to engage on the outstanding issues. The proposal stalled, and the opportunity was lost in 1993 when a new Greek-Cypriot government, formed by Glafcos Clerides in 1993, won a narrow victory campaigning on criticisms of the Ghali plan. Once more, the road forward was blocked.

The next few years showed little progress as Rauf Denktaş increasingly took a firm stance. He believed he had the power to obstruct Cyprus's entry into the EU, but he miscalculated. The EU was willing to move forward without Turkish-Cypriot support. Denktaş also lost his ally in Ankara. The AKP rose to power in Turkey in 2002 and looking for its own way into the EU was more open to a Cyprus solution than the hardliners in Ankara Denktaş had been accustomed to dealing with.

The UN would take one more swing at a Cyprus deal, its greatest in fifty years, but the two sides would never be as close to a solution as they were in the early nineties.

PART II

The EU Takes Charge

"Sir, it is worse than a crime, it is a blunder"

TALLEYRAND

CHAPTER 4

A New Influence

BEFORE EXAMINING THE European Union's role in Cyprus, it is worth stepping back and asking how it ever got involved in this minefield in the first place. After all, Cyprus has less than a million people and its membership was never going to substantially affect the lives of current EU citizens. So why even contemplate Cyprus as a member, given its history of intractable conflict?

One EU diplomat altruistically claimed that Cyprus was being considered as an EU member because it was in the islands' best interests. As this person pointed out, "Turk-Cypriots tell us that they do not want to be isolated. Young people on both sides in Cyprus want a solution and to join the EU." It was a noble sentiment. It was also revisionist history. The EU did not get involved to help the people of Cyprus.

The Turkish-Cypriot leader Denktaş claimed that the "EU wants Cyprus in its membership because of the geopolitical importance of

Cyprus. They want to extend their boundary east to influence the issue of petrol and to compete with the Americans for influence." This was certainly true, but the real driving reason was much simpler.

The EU was keen on accomplishing its fifth enlargement in 2004, and admitting Cyprus was necessary to muster the votes to bring nine other new nations into its ranks. Greece had threatened to veto the enlargement process unless Cyprus gained membership, divided or not. There were no subtleties about it. "If Cyprus is not admitted," said the Greek foreign minister, "then there will be no enlargement of the Community."

The EU capitulated to Greece's threatened veto rather than lose the opportunity to bring nine mostly Central European countries into the fold. It seemed a small price to pay. Leopold Maurer, the Cyprus head of the European Commission in Brussels, put it succinctly: "Member states like Germany were not interested in holding up enlargement of 100 million people because of 150,000 [Turkish-Cypriots]." In this manner, the EU assumed the primary role in resolving the Cyprus situation.

Having decided to proceed with Cyprus to protect enlargement, how well did the EU play its hand? Did it contribute to peace and progress, or the opposite?

Unfortunately for Cyprus, the EU, on balance, has played a very negative role on the island, and it started long before 2004. The EU should never have accepted the Cypriot application for membership in the first place. The Greek-Cypriots themselves were originally ambivalent about applying for EU membership, but intense lobbying by the Greeks in the period 1988-1990 convinced them to make the application. Effectively, this was a continuation of the Greek-Cypriot strategy of "internationalizing" the conflict in Cyprus. The Greeks turned away from the US as the "internationalizing" agent when the Americans did not give them their way. They then turned to the UN. When the UN began moving toward the Turkish position, says the University of Tubingen's Nathalie Tocci, Cyprus applied for membership in hopes of getting the EU involved on its side.

Initially, the EU declared that Cyprus would have to get its house in order before its membership would be considered. Paragraph 48 of a 1993 Commission opinion states that "as soon as the prospect of settlement is surer, the Commission is ready to start the process with Cyprus that should eventually lead to its accession."[34] By settlement, says Nanette Neuwahl of the University of Montreal's faculty of law, the European Commission was referring to "the question of the division of the island." There were three reasons for this stipulation:

1. European Community law and respect for human rights and fundamental freedoms could not be guaranteed on the whole island.
2. Accession without settlement would lead to inequality between the two parts of the island as economic disparity would increase.
3. Letting the Greek-Cypriot side into the EU on its own would bring de facto *taksim*, which is what the Turkish-Cypriots wanted all along.

34 Nathalie Tocci, "Cyprus and the European Union," *European Commission Opinion on the Application of Cyprus for Membership* (May, 1993): 4.

The original application had no impact on the Cypriot parties, contrary to the EU's hopes that it would serve as a catalyst to a settlement. The Turkish-Cypriots actually believed that their position was strengthened in that the Greek-Cypriots would now have to compromise on unity to get into the EU. They believed the Europeans main goal in accepting an application from Cyprus was to force an inter-communal settlement, and they took the EU at its word that membership would not be considered without a settlement. The EU should have known that it had given Turkish-Cypriots an effective veto on the nature of the settlement, making them less likely to compromise. Getting to a solution with only one side negotiating is virtually impossible.

The EU went ahead and accepted the Cyprus application anyway, which was legally dubious on a number of grounds. Says the British professor of international law, M. H. Mendelson: "The Greek-Cypriot administration is not entitled in international law to apply to join or join the European Union whilst Turkey is not a member. Greece and the United Kingdom are under obligation to prevent such accession."[35] Thus, two EU members, Greece, and the UK, having signed the Treaty of Guaranty, were in breach of international law by voting to accept the Cypriot application.

The EU was also offside because the Republic of Cyprus in Article 1 of the 1960 Treaty of Guarantee had bound itself "not to participate in whole or in part, in any political or economic

---

35   Nathalie Tocci, "The Cyprus Question," (Brussels: *CEPS Working Document* 154, September 2000), 36.

union with any State whatsoever."[36] (The late international relations expert Christopher Brewin dissents from this perspective,
stating that the "EU has the opinion of three international lawyers
that the government of the Republic of Cyprus is entitled to act
internationally.")[37]

The EU application also violated Cyprus's constitution, which
gives both the Greek-Cypriot president and Turkish-Cypriot vice-
president veto rights over foreign policy decisions. Leopold Maurer,
the head of the Cyprus team at the European Commission, argues
that, technically, there was no violation because the EU is not
a nation and "the Turkish-Cypriot Vice-President is not there to
veto." This is a convenient and naïve perspective. The EU may not
be a nation but the act of joining the EU is accomplished by vote
of individual member-nations of the EU, and these are clearly
nations. And while it was true that there was no Turkish-Cypriot
vice-president at the time of accession, this was only because
Makarios had unilaterally and illegally changed the Cypriot constitution to eliminate the vice-president while conducting the
genocide that we reviewed earlier.

The Turkish-Cypriots' explicit veto rights on major foreign policy
decisions had been granted in the 1960 constitution. An application to join the EU was obviously a major foreign policy decision,
and clearly qualified for a Turkish-Cypriot veto. There can be little

---

36   Stephen, *Perceptions*, 7.
37   Christopher Brewin, "Turkey, Greece and the European Union," in *Cyprus The Need for New Perspectives*, ed. Clement Dodd (Cambridgeshire: Eothen Press, 1999), 160.

doubt that if the Turkish-Cypriot vice-president had been in place, he would have exercised that veto on the Cyprus application.

The Greek-Cypriots never liked this Turkish-Cypriot veto but it was legal, and the EU decision to allow the Cyprus application without the agreement of the Turkish-Cypriots was in breach of both the letter and the spirit of Cypriot law. The fact that the EU and two of its members that were signatories to the Treaty of Guarantee were willing to turn a blind eye to the law did not reassure the Turks and Turkish-Cypriots that the EU was impartial or willing to live by the rule of law, and did not help the EU to play a positive role in Cyprus.

In the end, the EU's decision to accept the Cypriot application did not have the positive catalyst impact that the Greek-Cypriots, Greeks, and the Europeans wanted. It only hardened the Turkish-Cypriot stance. That was the EU's first mistake, one it was about to compound several times over.

Frustrated that the application to join the EU had not, on its own, led to a Cyprus solution, the Greeks pressured their EU colleagues to admit Cyprus even without coming to terms with the Turkish-Cypriots. As Nathalie Tocci explains, some clever diplomatic maneuvering allowed Cyprus to begin negotiations towards membership in return for Greece not blocking a Turkish-EU customs union. The pre-condition of a solution to the island's disunity was implicitly dropped. The deal was smoothed by side payments to Greek textile interests. The US encouraged the agreement, and many EU members, although dismayed at the prospect of admitting a divided Cyprus, reluctantly signed on, not wanting to endanger EU enlargement into Central and Eastern Europe.

The EU's new position, then, was a direct outcome of the Greek threat to veto EU enlargement. As the *Daily Telegraph* reported on August 15, 1996:

> The EU tends to be sympathetic to the Greek position, and has allowed Greek Cyprus to apply for membership on behalf of the whole island (a flagrant breach of the Cyprus constitution, which prohibits political or economic union with any other country) . . . The current unrest is aggravated by the Greek-Cypriot application to the EU which, on the proposed terms, would amount to *enosis* under any other name.

As a result of this second EU mistake, the Turkish-Cypriots lost what they thought was an effective veto in negotiations in Cyprus, one they could leverage toward their goal of *taksim* or partition. The pendulum swung to the other extreme, favouring the Greek maximalist position. As one of Denktaş's key advisors told us, "The EU was very naïve about the [Greek-Cypriots] entering the EU unilaterally. Basically, allowing them to join for all the island of Cyprus essentially gives the Greek-Cypriots the solution they wanted according to their parameters." This 1995 deal helped lead to the downfall of the Turkish government, which was viewed as soft on Cyprus. This lesson would not be lost on future Turkish politicians.

At the same time, EU meddling heightened expectations of Greek-Cypriots and led to demonstrations, the unrest mentioned by the *Telegraph*. In 1996, for the first time in over twenty years, Cypriots would die because of the conflict. Clearly, the EU's move to accept a divided Cyprus did not help the situation on the island, nor had it lessened Greek-Turkish tensions, which were further exacerbated by ongoing disputes over sovereignty and related concerns in the Aegean Sea.

In July 1997, the European Union's Agenda 2000 explicitly "allowed for the possibility of accession negotiations prior to a settlement" in Cyprus. Conditionality was formally renounced at the December 1999 Helsinki European Council, which stated that, "a political settlement will facilitate the accession of Cyprus to the European Union. If no settlement has been reached by the completion of the accession negotiations, the Council's decision on accession will be taken without the above being a precondition. In this the Council will take account of all relevant factors."[38]

The outcome of this second EU mistake was that the Greek-Cypriots no longer had an incentive to negotiate with their Turkish neighbours. They were going to be admitted even if they did not reach a solution. They would still have to play the game and pretend to negotiate so that they were not seen by the EU as the reluctant partner in the negotiations. As Nanette Neuwahl writes, the EU's offer to start accession talks enforced "the economic and strategic outlook" of Greek-Cyprus while also improving its diplomatic position.

Most EU diplomats we met with were quick to point out that Helsinki did not guarantee entry to Cyprus. "All relevant factors"

---

38   European Commission, *2001 Report on Cyprus' Progress towards Accession*, (Brussels: Commission of the European Communities SEC (2001) 1745, November 13, 2001), 20.

were to be considered in the final decision. Frankly, this was a fig leaf. As one senior diplomat in Cyprus said in 2002, "Cyprus will enter the EU in 2004. The train has left the station. [Cyprus president] Clerides would have to do something incredibly stupid to de-rail accession and he is too smart and won't do that."

One member of the European parliament tried to put a brave spin on the decision when we met in Brussels: "Turkey can't be a member for 10-15 years. Turkey said Cyprus would not come in until it did, which was not fair as it gave Turkey a veto on Cyprus accession. Allowing Cyprus in with no pre-conditions was good." There is an obvious double standard here. The EU felt it was unfair to allow the Turks a veto on the accession of Cyprus, but it was fine with allowing Greece or, in 2004, Cyprus, a nation with less than a million people, a veto on Turkey's EU admission.

Meanwhile, no progress was made toward unity in Cyprus. As the Turkish Business Association representative in Brussels, Bahadir Kaleagasi, correctly asserted, "The Greek-Cypriots don't negotiate because EU Enlargement Commissioner Gunter Verheugen has said that they can get in without negotiating anything. So why should they compromise?"

With these first two major mistakes, the EU failed to create an environment which might lead to compromise, but its biggest error in the entire process was yet to come. The EU summit in Luxembourg in 1997 agreed to proceed with the eleven-country enlargement of the EU, but completely ignored and excluded Turkey. Said the Commission in Agenda 2000: "Turkey was treated differently from all other applicant countries in that no recommendation was made for accession or pre-accession strategies." The

reason given was "primarily political grounds." As the journalist
Christian de Bellaigue wrote:

> The summit declaration excluded Turkey from the eleven-
> country enlargement process (which included, humiliatingly,
> the former Ottoman territory of Bulgaria) and gave indi-
> rect backing for Greece's position on bilateral disputes with
> Turkey—a violation of a 1975 European Council undertaking
> that Greece's membership would "not affect relations between
> the Community and Turkey."[39]

One month after Luxembourg, the EU added salt to Turkey's wound
by beginning negotiations with Cyprus. The EU had now placed
itself in a situation where neither side had any incentive to negotiate.
The Turks had wanted to join the EU. They now had little hope of
membership. That destroyed what little leverage the EU had over
Turkey and Denktaş and the Turkish-Cypriots, and the prospects
for peace diminished considerably. The US had lobbied intensely
to prevent this mistake from happening—assistant secretary of state
Richard Holbrooke was furious that the EU had snubbed a key
ally—but in the end it was the EU's decision to make.

Virtually all EU officials we spoke to agreed, off the record,
that Luxembourg had been a disaster and probably the low point
in the Cyprus admission process. Most critically, the EU action in
Luxembourg exacerbated already tense EU-Turkey relations.

---

39   Christopher de Bellaigue, "Conciliation in Cyprus," *Washington Quarterly* (Spring
     1999), 189.

The EU's fourth significant mistake was its failure to position itself as an objective mediator in Cyprus. Virtually from the start, it had acted as an advocate for the Greek-Cypriots. This was perhaps inevitable, given that Greece was a member and Turkey was not, but the EU could still have played a more effective role. It could have learned from the American experience in the Middle East, where successive administrations have been ineffective in part because they were not perceived as objective middle parties, given their constant siding with Israel.

Several actions by the EU helped confirm its anti-Turkish bias in the minds of many observers. It did not recognize the two parties to the Cyprus dispute as equals, a grave error that has impeded every stage of discussions. This attitude can be seen as far back as 1983, when the Turkish Republic of Northern Cyprus was formed. The EU reaction was: "The commission deeply regrets and rejects the unilateral declaration of independence of the Turkish-Cypriot community. The Government of Cyprus is the sole legitimate representative recognized by the European community."[40]

The fact is that the current government of Cyprus is illegitimate according to the 1960 constitution because of unilateral constitutional changes (without required Turkish-Cypriot consent) imposed by Greek-Cypriots. All the EU offices are in the southern or Greek part of Cyprus, and most EU officials treat the TRNC as they would a rebellious child. They fail to appreciate the history that has led to the current impasse and fault only

40   Bulletin of the European Commission, No. 11, 1983 point 2.2.34

the Turkish-Cypriots. Given the ethnic cleansing and unilateral, illegal Greek-Cypriot actions during the 1960s and 70s, we would argue that the Greek-Cypriots bear more responsibility than the Turkish-Cypriots. Finger pointing, however, does not help. In the end, both parties are guilty, both were intransigent at different points in time, and both contributed to this mess. Failing to treat the parties as equals has seriously undermined EU credibility on the Turkish side.

EU credibility was also damaged by failure to insist that the Turkish-Cypriots be involved in the EU accession discussions. "It was not up to me," one senior EU official admitted, "but we should have involved the Turkish-Cypriots much more in the negotiations to enter the EU." The Europeans were extremely naïve about the implications of asking the Greek-Cypriots alone to negotiate for membership. One of the most pro-Greek-Cypriot EU diplomats we spoke to confessed that the "EU should have pushed much harder at the beginning to get the Turkish-Cypriots involved in a meaningful way in the accession discussions. They could have leaned harder on the Greek-Cypriots who only offered token participation. The Greek-Cypriots made the Turkish-Cypriots an offer that they knew the Turkish-Cypriots would have to refuse."

Token participation was not consistent with the Turkish-Cypriot right to participate in major foreign policy decisions based on the 1960 constitution. As Denktaş lamented, "the EU blames me for intransigence. They all applauded when Clerides invited Turkish-Cypriots to take part in the EU accession discussions. The British Prime Minister applauded Clerides. But I said no because it put us in the position of the minority, not as a partner, which violates the 1960 agreements."

So, yes, the Turkish-Cypriots *should* have been involved in more than a token way, but why would the Greek-Cypriots allow them to be? The EU did not require Turkish-Cypriots to be involved, and Cyprus was going to get into the EU, anyway.

The many EU statements supportive of Greek-Cypriots also cost them support amongst the Turkish-Cypriots. Virtually every week during the accession negotiations some EU diplomat or an EU country senior politician would marvel at how supportive and flexible the Greek-Cypriots were. They kept reminding everyone that the Greek-Cypriots were going to be admitted, which, apart from discouraging the Greek-Cypriots from negotiating, damaged the EU in the eyes of the Turkish-Cypriots.

These same officials either failed to mention the Turkish-Cypriots altogether or, if they did rate a mention, delivered a diplomatic, and sometimes not so diplomatic slap in the face. Every major diplomatic figure in Nicosia and in Brussels claimed that Clerides moved considerably but Denktaş had not. These statements combined with constant reminders from Prodi, the EU president, Joschka Fischer, the German foreign minister, and Verheugen, the EU enlargement commissioner, amongst others, that Cyprus was getting in. This was not the help negotiators needed to get to a deal on the island.

Verheugen, in particular, harmed the process by continuously cheering for one side. On March 7, 2002 *The Guardian* carried the headline, "EU Commission says Cypriot accession will proceed regardless of settlement." In mid-April 2002, the *Cyprus Weekly* quoted Verheugen as saying that there was less than a 50 percent chance that the talks would succeed this year "because the Turkish side refused to budge." He went on to say that the Greek-Cypriot side was showing a "positive and constructive approach to the process." One Turkish politician, Nationalist Movement Party (MHP) leader Sadi Somuncuoglu, said that Verheugen had "committed a crime" when he said that the north, or Turkish Cyprus, would be EU territory. Clearly, the EU enlargement commissioner was uninterested in positioning himself as an objective observer of the negotiation process.

EU credibility further suffered amongst the Turkish-Cypriots when the northern part of the island did not get its fair share of EU grants and loans. Most of the infrastructure projects were directed to the south. Prodded by the Greeks, the EU passed a rule prohibiting the acceptance of goods coming from Cyprus if they did not have certificates from the Republic of Cyprus (the Greek-Cypriot south). This effectively banned Turkish-Cypriot goods from the EU. As Nathalie Tocci says, "the international community has fuelled the dynamics of the conflict by widening the economic disparities between northern and southern regions."[41] Adds de Bellaigue, "Many Turkish-Cypriots reserve a special bitterness for what they see as European perfidy. To uncover the reason, ask Turkish-Cypriots about the 1994 ruling of the European Court of Justice that effectively banned EU countries from buying perishable goods from Northern Cyprus."[42]

41   Tocci, *The Cyprus Question*, 12.
42   De Bellaigue, *Conciliation in Cyprus*, 191.

Not surprisingly, Turkish-Cypriot political parties that were pro-Europe saw their share of the vote drop from 46 percent to 31 percent between 1985 and 1998. As the British high commissioner in Cyprus told us in 2002, "there has been a demonization of the EU in the north [of Cyprus], which probably dates to the point when the Turkish-Cypriots were excluded from the accession discussions."

CHAPTER 5

Why did the EU do what it did?

I T IS ONE THING to note the critical mistakes highlighted in the last chapter, and another to explain why the EU failed to play an effective and positive role in Cyprus. We believe there are three principal reasons for the mistakes: international decision lock-in; the EU's foreign policy processes; and a general failure to understand history, and the bias that flows from that failure.

The EU did not inherit a fresh problem when it was handed the Cyprus file in the early 1990s. As we have seen, the tensions date from 1963. Way back then, the international community started making decisions it would find difficult, if not impossible, to reverse later. The EU inherited some of these locked-in positions, many of which hampered the effort to find a just and equitable solution in Cyprus.

The most egregious lock-in was the fact that the international community did not accept the two parties to the dispute as equals. The EU did not invent this failure. As the British international relations expert Christopher Brewin argues, "The UN just cannot accept that it made an unjust and unwise decision in 1964 to recognize the Greek-Cypriot administration as the legitimate government of the Republic of Cyprus."[43] Its early decision to deny Turkish-Cypriot equality, notwithstanding the 1960 constitution, was perpetuated in all subsequent talks launched by the UN. The EU, in turn, accepted the UN view of Cyprus, as did the rest of the international community. The result has been an absence of a truly balanced mediator in the Cyprus saga.

The other serious lock-in decision by the international community was to consider partition an illegitimate option. This decision was effectively taken first by the British in the late 1950s as they ended their colonial rule. Partition had been discussed partly to keep the Turkish-Cypriots on the side of the British while Greek-Cypriots fought for independence. When trouble broke out in 1963, partition was floated again as an option by the Americans but the Greek-Cypriots would not accept it unless forced to do so, as they were a decade later in 1974. The international community reiterated its opposition to partition after the Turks imposed it militarily, but this, again, was a repetition of what had become conventional wisdom with respect to Cyprus.

43 Clement Dodd, "Postscript," in *Cyprus The Need for New Perspectives*, ed. Clement Dodd (Cambridgeshire: Eothen Press, 1999), 316.

The international community's thinking at least had the virtue of consistency. At the end of the Second World War, there were only two micro states (those with populations of less than one million) in the world: Luxembourg and Iceland. In 1960, UN General Assembly resolutions 1514 and 1541 recognized the right to self-determination only for colonial peoples. There was no residual right of self-determination for minority peoples within new states. Using this metric, the UN could have opposed new states for the Tamils in Sri Lanka or the Eritreans in Ethiopia. They did, in fact, oppose a move for a separate Ibo state of Biafra. The international community, including the EU (for obvious reasons given the issues in Spain, France and Northern Ireland) continues to prefer not to see states divided. Thus, the EU warned the Czechs and Slovaks that their future prospects depended on the continuing integrity of Czechoslovakia. This bluff was called and since both countries were eventually admitted, it shows that the EU would be willing to back down if the Cypriots in the future agreed to a deal that was similar to what happened with the Czechs and Slovaks. They should have been willing to consider this option in the lead-up to 2004.

The world has changed since Cyprus descended into chaos fifty-nine years ago. In 2001, there were forty-five microstates. This change in international thinking was essentially driven by the implosion of the Soviet Union. The EU was quick to recognize the new ex-Soviet republics:

On 16 December 1991, the European Community's Council of Ministers adopted the 'Declaration on Guidelines on the Recognition of New States in Eastern Europe and the Soviet

Union' and agreed to extend recognition by 15 January 1992 to those republics that met the conditions of recognition. . . . It then noted that the European Community would "recognize subject to normal standards of international practice and political realities in each case, those new states which, following the historic changes in the region, have constituted themselves on a democratic basis, have accepted the appropriate international obligations and have committed themselves in good faith to a peaceful process and to negotiations."[44]

The demise of the communist systems of Central and Eastern Europe changed the climate around the rights of self-determination for peoples trapped amid what they consider foreign states. "The world's leading powers, fatigued and exasperated by what often appears to be longstanding, irrational blood feuds among former partners and neighbours, have shown a growing tendency to acquiesce in the forcible separation of ethnic groups for the sake of preserving regional peace,"[45] says professor Tozun Bahcheli of the University of Western Ontario.

Unfortunately for the Turkish-Cypriots, the international willingness to accept self-determination came after the world had already locked into what it perceived to be the right answer for Cyprus. Had the ethnic cleansing happened in 2002 or today instead of 1963, the international community would most probably

44   European Commission: Europa.eu.int – Relations with Cyprus
45   Tozun Bahchelli and Nicolas Rizopoulos, "The Cyprus Impasse: What next?," *World Policy Journal* (Winter 1996), 3.

have demanded ethnic separation as a means of keeping the peace and saving lives. The only difference between Cyprus and the former Soviet Union is that one former parent, the USSR, accepted the right of self-determination for its ethnically distinct nations. The Greek-Cypriots have never been so accommodating. George Vassiliou, former president of Cyprus, insisted, "we cannot and will not accept self-determination. It would be a very dangerous precedent if I were to agree to this, every community, every ethnic group in the world would demand it."[46]

Vassiliou was right that many ethnic groups would demand it, but is this really a bad solution? If people of a different ethnicity vote democratically to form their own nation, why should the international community not respect that voice?

The separation of warring ethnic groups was also the solution that the international community, and the EU, devised for Bosnia. US Assistant Secretary of State Richard Holbrooke speculated that the Bosnian model might work for Cyprus. The de facto partition of Cyprus since 1974 has been successful at least in terms of lives lost. The separation is clearly not perfect, but it is preferable to the persistent conflict elsewhere in the Middle East.

Why has the international community rejected partition as a long-term answer in Cyprus and instead insisted on forcing a solution which has repeatedly failed? Why the double standard? As several Cypriot experts say,

46   Mary Anne Weaver, "Report from Cyprus," *New Yorker*, August 6, 1990, 75.

The Turkish Cypriots, whose Turkish forbears colonized the island in 1571 . . . have long established stake in Cyprus and cannot be dismissed as '400-year visitors.' They, too, claim the right of self-determination, which lies at the heart of liberal democracy and which is very difficult to deny, however politically disruptive it may be in some parts of the world. If Kosovo and East Timor, they ask, why not Northern Cyprus? This is what lies at the heart of the Cyprus conflict, nullifying so far attempts to unite the two sides politically.[47]

Nanette Neuwahl describes the difference in the handling of Kosovo and North Cyprus: "Whereas the former was met with collective intervention, the latter mainly gave rise to passive criticism."[48] That passive criticism is a direct consequence of decision lock-in.

* * *

The EU's process for making foreign policy decisions deserve much of the blame for the way the Cyprus file has been handled. The twenty-eight countries of the EU are divided north vs south, big countries vs small countries, and old guard vs new entrants (mostly from Eastern Europe). Larger, richer, northern countries that originally formed the EU would like the others to tag along, but that

47 Andrew Mango, Christian Heinze, Clement Dodd, Ergun Olgun, Georges Delcoigne and Paul Taylor, "The Need for New Perspectives on Cyprus," *Center for the Study of International Relations and Strategic Studies* (Brussels: February 15, 2000), 16.
48 Neuwahl, *Cyprus Which Way*, 5.

has not happened. As Peter Preston wrote in the *Guardian*, "we talk about the development of a European foreign policy so that we may lecture the Israelis or the Japanese or the Brazilians on the folly of their ways. It is inflated garbage. Europe lacks both the will and the clout to meet a challenge gnawing at its own entrails. The failure is abject."[49]

The failure to meet the challenge acute on files like Cyprus because of the lack of consensus and the relative unimportance of the issue. Looking at EU decisions on these two dimensions—consensus and urgency—helps to explain where it often goes off the rails. When issues are important and there is a high degree of consensus for action within the EU, it can be effective, as has been seen in recent trade disputes and in its handling of competitive issues such as the Google file. The EU also can be effective when there is strong consensus on less important issues such as EU relations with distant countries (Venezuela, for instance). When an issue is important but there is a weak consensus in the EU, as with respect to Turkey's application to join the EU, it inevitably ends up in gridlock. The high importance of the issue leaves opposed parties reluctant to move to consensus.

Cyprus falls into the fourth category of decisions at the EU, those where there is weak consensus and not much at stake, at least as far as most of its members are concerned. Issues of this sort often produce a lot of noise, but almost no movement, validating Sayre's law, named after the American political scientist Wallace Sayre: "In

---

49   Peter Preston, "A tragedy of two races: Problem of Cyprus will blight Euro plans for Enlargement," *The Guardian*, October 26, 1998.

any dispute, the intensity of feeling is inversely proportional to the value of the issues at stake."

Most European partners did not want to admit a divided Cyprus to its ranks, and those attitudes persist. France, Germany, Italy, and Holland repeatedly called for a political settlement prior to Cyprus' EU accession, writes Nathalie Tocci, but none of those members were prepared to go to the wall for Cyprus. The issue was not crucial to any EU member but Greece, and so Greece could hijack the EU decision-making process and frustrate the (weak) will of its larger membership.

Greece, despite promising at the time of its own accession to the EU that it would not use its veto against Turkey, has effectively used the threat of holding up EU enlargement to get what it wants on Cyprus. One observer puts it more forcefully: "The Greeks are cheerfully using their position inside the European Economic Community to blackmail the Turks over Cyprus." That Greece is using blackmail to get its way is perhaps to be expected, but it is intolerable that the rest of the EU has capitulated to its behavior.

Another problem with EU policy processes is that the institution's size and diversity render it inflexible. "The EU cannot manage foreign policy in a subtle way," says one senior diplomat. "This is a heterogeneous body that resembles a supertanker. It can't be manoeuvred gently."

Unlike the United States, which has one foreign policy and the means to deliver, the EU faces enormous challenges in bringing its members around to a coherent view. The result is a complex and ponderous mess of a decision-making process as explained by Charlotte Bretherton and John Vogler in *The EU as a Global Actor*:

[The EU] tends to be slow to take up positions and, once taken, they are difficult to amend. This is a structural consequence of the Union's internal decision-making procedures, which in effect adds an extra layer of political complexity (even when there is community competence). The negotiator has no single constituency but 15 [original EU members], along with the normal special interests and, indeed, the Commission itself. It is, in the circumstances, not surprising that the EU/EC can be a ponderous negotiating partner deficient in the flexibility that may be required to arrive at a speedy conclusion.[50]

With a certain measure of diplomatic subtlety, the EU might have brought Cyprus to a lasting peace. It had the means to force agreement, thanks to the high interest of both Cyprus and Turkey in joining the EU. But the EU did not behave that way. Instead, it continually sent mixed and at times ambiguous signals regarding Cyprus, as one might expect given that the EU's foreign policy reflected its own bureaucrats plus fifteen countries' foreign ministers and heads of state. Even while the EU was toeing the party line that a divided Cyprus would easily be admitted, two of its members voicing their contradictory opinions publicly. In 1999, French Foreign Minister Hubert Vedrine said that the admission of a divided Cyprus "would cause enormous problems, most notably the reinforcement of divisions. One needs to distinguish between the opening of discussions and the negotiations, which highlight

---

50   Charlotte Bretherton and John Vogler, *The European Union as a Global Actor* (London: Routledge, 1999), 252.

problems which we will need to deal with and the conclusion."[51]
Similarly, after the EU had admitted a divided Cyprus, British
Foreign Secretary Malcolm Rifkind said, "Without a unified
Cyprus, the problem of accession to the European Union will be
extremely difficult, and very difficult to realize."[52]

Those are but two of many examples of mixed and conflicting
signals sent by the EU and its members. All states face this problem
of speaking with one voice, but to the EU these problems grow
exponentially, and the situation is worse today with its membership having expanded from fifteen to twenty-eight often-divergent
views. Sometimes the EU winds up arguing with itself in its own
reports, as it did in late 1998 when it wrote that it "regrets the
statements of 9 Nov 98 by some EU member states opposing EU
membership of Cyprus unless the partition is ended, because this
weakens the EU common foreign policy and the catalyst role the
accession process could play in solving the Cyprus problem."[53]
These flaws in EU communication have compounded the difficulties around Cyprus, as each side has tended to listen to the
perspective it wanted to hear.

The EU decision-making process also suffers from what we
would term a snowball phenomenon. This is acute on files which
are not viewed as important by most EU members. In these cases,
EU bureaucrats—even less accountable to elected officials than

51 www.pio.cy/news/dailynews/new 1999_5_17.htm
52 *Cyprus Mail*, November 29, 1996.
53 European Commission, *Resolution on the Regular Report from the Commission on
    Cyprus progress towards accession*, Brussels: (COM(98)0710-C4-0108/99),5.

is true in most nations because of the low legitimacy of elected European members of parliament—are in control. Once the bureaucrats take on a file, it develops a life of its own. They work independently of member nations and elected officials, and before anyone has noticed, they've rolled the snowball downhill to the point where it becomes unstoppable—an avalanche. Such was the case with Cyprus. Says Rauf Denktaş:

> In the 1992 Set of Ideas, Vassiliou wanted to insert a clause about Cyprus' pursuing the application to join the EU. I said no, only after we had reached a settlement should we pursue membership. Then they applied and the British told us "don't worry – it may be in the mail but it won't be processed." Then they started to process the Cyprus application and the British told us "don't worry this will take a very long time." Then, in 1995 when it speeded up the British said "well, we couldn't sit on it forever."

The EU did not think that letting Cyprus apply in the first place would be a problem because it would not admit Cyprus divided. Then the bureaucrats got involved. Once they waived settlement as a pre-condition, the snowball gathered speed. Cyprus was suddenly a candidate for membership, and it was on a timetable towards a decision on its admission. There came a point where the EU, following the letter of the Helsinki decision, should have declared the Greek-Cypriots not to be negotiating in good faith and declined its application, but by that point the snowball was huge, and the avalanche was inevitable. A rejection would have prompted Greece to hold up enlargement. A minor issue, Cyprus, could not be allowed to impact a major EU initiative, enlargement. Of course, the avalanche should have been predicted the moment the Cyprus application was filed in the early 1990s.

The EU is not strong at evaluating the long-term consequences of its decisions, especially those that seem minor at first glance. This was evident to one Turkish politician back in 2002: "The EU has the luxury of leaving strategic thinking to the US. They are free wheeling and not thinking about long-term consequences of their current plan to let South Cyprus in."

"In essence," write Charlotte Bretherton and John Vogler, "the decision-making procedures constructed to meet the needs of . . . member states across a relatively limited range of policy areas have been the subject of incremental reform rather than fundamental reformulation."[54] With the addition of new members joining since 2002, the situation at the EU has only gotten worse. If the errors of Cyprus are to be avoided in the future, it needs to overhaul its decision-making process, re-establish accountability to member nations, and eliminate vetoes by individual members.

* * *

In their classic *Thinking in Time,* Richard Neustadt and Ernest May preach the importance of understanding history to avoid enormous political blunders. They emphasize the need to know

---

54   Bretherton and Vogler, *European Union,* 9.

the full story. "Start the story as far back as it properly goes," they write, "and plot key trends while also entering key events, especially big changes. Don't foreshorten the history in ways that may distort it."[55]

The international community, including the EU, disregards this advice, and its ignorance of the history of Cyprus has led to poor decisions. Most EU decision makers, with the exception of Britain and Greece, only heard about Cyprus in 1974 when the Turks invaded. The history of Cyprus, for them, begins in 1974, which is convenient for Greece and the Greek-Cypriots, and unfortunate for the Turkish side. Most observers we talked to were vaguely aware of distant atrocities committed against Turkish-Cypriots, but these crimes did not have the impact of more recent events in the former Yugoslavia. One senior EU Member of Parliament proudly told us that the EU was not fooled by Cyprus: "People on the island are in a bad way because of the division of the island." The statement suggests all was well until the Turks intervened in 1974. That was clearly not the case.

Had the EU better understood the history of Cyprus and of Turkey back in 2002, it wouldn't have leaned on the cynical tactic of throwing money at the Turks. "Denktaş is not motivated by the economic carrots the EU has dangled," one senior diplomat in Nicosia told us. "[European commissioner for enlargement] Verheugen promised 200 million Euros to the north which his people would love but that does not drive Denktaş." The Turkish-Cypriots had suffered

---

55   Richard Neustadt and Ernest May, *Thinking in Time* (New York: The Free Press, 1986), 236.

hardships through twenty-seven years of an economic blockade. That should have been sufficient to convince the EU that Turkey and the Turkish-Cypriots would not be motivated by economic considerations alone. The peoples' pride was more important, and any reading of history would confirm this. Unfortunately, the EU constantly assaulted Turkish pride.

Understanding history would also have emphasized the importance of security rather than economic benefit to the Turkish-Cypriots, especially to the older decision makers who came of age politically in the 1960s and 1970s. Like most leaders in Israel, these veterans had witnessed genocide and no amount of money would tempt them to be put back in harm's way. Security and national pride should have been emphasized by the EU but, instead, these were underplayed due to this fundamental failure to understand history.

One issue alone should convince the reader of the EU's insensitivity to history and national pride. Verheugen said that Cyprus could be admitted into the EU in Athens in early 2003, during Greece's turn as president of the EU. So, Cyprus would be admitted with a signing at the Parthenon in Athens. How would Turkish-Cypriots, who would have been present if a deal in Cyprus had been reached, have felt about a ceremony that would have effectively labelled them as losers and Greece as the winners? One can understand why the Greeks wanted this, but why would the EU have allowed it? How insensitive could the EU have been? Leopold Maurer of the EU defended the signing by saying that it "was a coincidence as the Greek Presidency was decided five years ago." This is hard to credit given Verheugen's stand, but surely the

EU should have been savvy enough to understand the need to avoid a symbolic insult to the Turkish side.

A large part of the EU's ineffectiveness in Cyprus is because of institutional and personal bias rooted in a misreading of history. "The bureaucrats are biased," one analyst who deals with virtually all the key players in Brussels told us flatly. And the bureaucrats are hardly alone. Again in 2002, Thomas Weston, the US state department's Cyprus envoy, said after his meeting with President Clerides, "we had one of our continuing excellent meetings about the status of the talks. As always it was very satisfactory from our point of view."[56] The *Cyprus Mail* added, "he made no such statements after his lunchtime meeting with Turkish-Cypriot leader Rauf Denktaş whom he only thanked for continuing with the direct talks at this stage." When diplomats like Mr. Weston have already made up their minds, it is virtually impossible for the Turkish-Cypriots to be properly heard.

There are countless other examples of the international community's bias in dealing with the Turks. The Turks, for instance, noticed that the EU required that problems between Hungary and Romania be solved before accession negotiations for those nations began, a requirement waived for Cyprus. This bias was evident to a peacekeeper forty years ago. The Greek-Cypriots were very friendly and frankly very European. We saw them as being very much like us. The Turkish side was forbidding; in many ways, it felt like crossing the former Iron Curtain. The Turkish-Cypriots and the Turks

---

56   Annie Charalambous, "Settlement feasible by June – Weston," *Cyprus Weekly*, March 15-21, 2002.

treated us as though we were the enemy. We did not socialize with the Turks; they shunned us, and we reciprocated. Very quickly, all of my UN colleagues adopted a pro-Greek tilt. Our congenial staff were Greek-Cypriots. Inevitably, all problems were blamed on the Turkish-Cypriots.

This same bias continues today. All the international diplomats and the EU personnel are based in Greek Cyprus. They too become close friends with these wonderful people and it colours their view of the problem. The Turkish-Cypriots have not helped their cause by gratuitously insulting EU personnel or by making visits and travel difficult. The Greek-Cypriots, by contrast, have handled their public relations brilliantly. The Greek-Cypriots repeat their mantras: "yes, there were problems pre-1974, but there were atrocities on both sides." And, "yes, some mistakes were made, but mostly by fanatics or by the Greeks themselves, primarily the past military junta." The Turks prefer to let the historical facts speak for themselves, but this is a useless public relations tactic given that most of the international community does not really understand the history of the island.

"The EU still holds Turkey solely responsible for the situation in Cyprus,"[57] concluded the late scholar Clement Dodd. This misreading of history goes a long way towards explaining the EU's ineffectiveness. The equivalent would be for some Middle East middleman trying to bring peace to that troubled land to misapprehend either the injustice done to the Palestinians by the

57 Dodd, *New Perspectives*, 303.

1917 Balfour Declaration or the genocide against the Jews in the Holocaust. Failure to understand the full dimensions of history leads to unwarranted bias and stands in the way of acceptable and lasting solutions, as the EU, by now, should have learned.

CHAPTER 6

What the EU Wrought

HAVING REVIEWED THE European Union's mishandling of Cyprus, and explored some of the reasons behind it, we now turn to the consequences. One, certainly, has been a loss of legitimacy in Brussels. The EU exposed itself as a poor mediator and harmed its long-term diplomatic capabilities by allowing Greece and the Greek-Cypriots to hijack its proceedings.

The EU could have avoided this outcome by studying what had happened in NATO. Monteagle Stearns, former US ambassador to Greece, said that in his experience, the Greeks are "often disposed to introduce bilateral problems into the military business of the alliance." He added that "had NATO been more conscious of the divisive effects Greek-Turkish differences would have on the alliance's future position in the eastern Mediterranean and more willing to make full membership contingent on settling them, much of the later trouble might have been avoided."[58]

This example should have prompted EU members, who saw what happened in NATO from the inside, to avoid the alliance's error. It did not, and the outcome was foreseeable, as political scientist Stephen Larrabee demonstrated at the time:

> Rather than facilitating a Cyprus settlement, as the policy was intended to do, the EU's decision to open accession negotiations with the Greek part of Cyprus prior to an overall political settlement threatens to lead to a hardening of the status quo and de facto partition of the island. Moreover, the decision could have serious consequences for the EU itself, resulting in the importation of an explosive dispute into the EU's midst, which could seriously paralyze its internal decision-making process.[59]

The very ideals of the EU are now under threat thanks to the entry of a divided Cyprus. "The Enlightenment ideal of republican constitutions protecting the equality and freedom of all citizens under the law, and the establishment of a league of liberal states is undermined in all its essentials by the Cyprus conflict,"[60] writes Christopher Brewin.

---

58 Stearns, *Entangled Allies*, 76.
59 Stephen Larrabee, "US and European Perspectives on the Eastern Mediterranean," Paper presented at *Rhodes Conference*, June 5-6, 1998, 11.
60 Brewin in Dodd, Cyprus *The Need for New Perspectives*, 168.

Brewin also notes that the ill-fated 2004 decision to admit Cyprus was of huge consequence for both Cyprus and Turkey: "The spectacular progress of the Republic of Cyprus towards accession has been achieved at a substantial cost in worsening the prospects for a settlement, and increasing the likelihood of a war between Greece and Turkey. EU relations with Turkey have been seriously damaged."[61]

The EU's Helsinki decision to renounce the settlement requirement before granting membership to Cyprus all but guaranteed the outcome of its proceedings would be no solution (and continued division), or a bad solution. Again, this was evident at the time. Ozdem Sanberk of the Istanbul-based research organization TESEV said in 2002, "My feeling is that the talks will break down, not definitely, but there will be some kind of crisis."[62] Professor Heinz-Jurgen Axt of the University of Duisburg-Essen added, "the best scenario for Cyprus' EU membership—solution of the conflict between the two communities first and then subsequent entry to the EU—is the least probable of all to be realized."[63]

After Helsinki, both sides in Cyprus were more interested in the perception of movement and progress than they were in actual progress. Greek-Cypriots believed they would gain entry so long as they were not to blame for any gridlock. Turkish-Cypriots felt

61   Brewin in Dodd, Cyprus *The Need for New Perspectives*, 148.
62   Gareth Jones, "Cems slams 'biased' EU over Cyprus," *Cyprus Mail*, March 26, 2002.
63   Heinz-Jurgen Axt, "The Island of Cyprus and the European Union," in *Cyprus The Need for New Perspectives*, ed. Clement Dodd (Cambridgeshire: Eothen Press, 1999), 174.

betrayed by the entire process, and the Turks lost any incentive to compromise when the EU shelved its membership application.

Instead of sincere efforts, each side now sought to avoid blame the other for the eventual failure of settlement talks. "Enough of the military and government in Ankara have decided that the past policies have not worked and so they want to at least appear to be cooperative," one diplomat told us. "They want to make sure that if these discussions fail, they cannot be blamed." Greek Prime Minister Costas Simitis echoed this view, "Denktaş's decision to attend new talks was merely a tactical maneuver by the Turkish side to appease the EU and demonstrate good intentions."[64] Greece was toying with the process, as well, but a quick review of international media reaction shows the blame falling on the Turks, who may have been guilty, but not alone.

Far from acting as a catalyst for peace, the EU's misbegotten diplomatic process pushed the sides further apart. "There has been a steady deterioration of the conflict," Nathalie Tocci wrote in 2002. The EU's policies "may be indeed 'catalytic,' but towards crisis rather than settlement."[65] Once a Cypriot settlement was waived as a condition of entry, the Greek-Cypriots took several deliberate steps that made a solution less likely. They launched numerous legal actions against Turkish-Cypriots in the European Court of Human Rights. For example, on July 29, 1998, in Loizidou vs. Turkey, the court ruled that Turkey had to pay compensation for unjustified denial of access to property owned by a Greek-Cypriot (Loizidou)

---

64 *Cyprus Weekly*, February 22-28, 2002.
65 Tocci, *Cyprus and the European Union*, 1.

in the northern city of Kyrenia. The same court also ruled in favour of Cyprus 16-1 in finding Turkey guilty of human rights abuses in Cyprus. What purpose did these cases serve? Each revolved around central issues that were being negotiated between the Greek and Turkish Cypriots. They should have been subject to compromise rather than legal arbitrage. The net result of the Greek-Cypriot legal campaign was to reduce the prospects for peace and, again, it was a foreseeable outcome of the EU's approach to the island.

The Greek-Cypriots also became increasingly belligerent once the EU took the reins in Cyprus. They spent $325 million on defense in 1990, which was three times what they had spent in 1986. This did nothing for the prospects for peace. In 1997, after conditionality of a settlement had been waived, the Greek-Cypriots threatened to deploy S-300 missiles in Cyprus (Turkey reacted so negatively that the missiles were instead deployed in Crete). In April 1998, the Greek air force opened an air base in Paphos (Cyprus), extending the range of Greek aircraft to the southern coast of Turkey. And by 1997, the Greek-Cypriots had acquired 140 tanks (up from ten in 1985) as they moved to close the military gap with the north.

These measures were never going to eliminate the gap with the north, as Turkey could still quickly overwhelm Cyprus if it chose, but they did undermine peace. In 2002, President Denktaş sketched a scenario deeply disturbing to Turkish-Cypriots. With South Cyprus representing the whole island in the EU, the Greek-Cypriots could "claim that Turkey is occupying EU land and get the EU involved. Then the issue will boil within the EU and upset Greek-Turkey and EU-Turkey relations . . . The Greek-Cypriots will play games as they did before. They will cause incidents and can be militarily strong enough to hold off Turkey for a week to ten days, then the EU will get dragged in. They [the Greeks] are very imaginative."

Outside observers, too, fully expected the Greek-Cypriots to use the EU to internationalize their conflict. "The Cypriot Foreign Minister told German Foreign Minister Fischer when he was in Bonn that the Greek-Cypriots would not import the Cyprus problem in to the EU if Cyprus was admitted divided," one diplomat reported. "All of us know in practice that in such a case we would, in fact, be importing the Cyprus problem into the EU."

The new vulnerability of the Turkish-Cypriots prompted them to accept more Turkish protection, and shifted the focus from the diplomatic arena, where efforts should have been concentrated, to military affairs. These outcomes, too, were obvious as they were happening. "The question has to be asked whether Greece and the Republic of Cyprus in their efforts to internationalize the Cyprus issue through application to the EU and through the planned introduction of the missiles have not ruined all chances of an agreement on the island,"[66] said Clement Dodd at the time.

The Turkish side did make efforts to alert the international community to the fraudulence of the EU process. In a March 2002 speech, Turkish Foreign Minister Ismail Cem said:

---

66 Clement Dodd, "Cyprus in Turkish Politics and Foreign Policy,' in *Cyprus The Need for New Perspectives*, ed. Clement Dodd (Cambridgeshire: Eothen Press, 1999), 144.

I am not sure that the EU is doing its best to support the peace process in Cyprus. Remarks are being made in the EU that encourage the Greek-Cypriots to be more intransigent, saying that whatever you do over there, don't worry. It won't affect your membership chances. I am afraid the Greek-Cypriots are not very inclined, and have no incentive, to respond to the Turkish-Cypriot proposals. If a mutually acceptable solution is not reached . . . then we will have difficulties. The EU has a legal and moral obligation to both nations of Cyprus . . . the EU should be more energetic and stop telling only the Turkish-Cypriot side to find a solution.[67]

Denktaş added:

After [Cypriot president] Clerides won the election, I wanted to talk to him but he said there were no common grounds for discussions and when I mentioned the Set of Ideas, he said he did not want to hear about this Set of Ideas. EU accession is preventing a settlement. Mr. Clerides no longer favours a federation as seen in the Set of Ideas. The Set of Ideas foresaw that we would be separate, that the three freedoms would be restricted, that there would be bi-zonality and that the outside power guarantee would stand. Clerides does not support these ideas now because he can get into EU without giving any of these, which are necessary to re-establish the partnership that was broken in 1963.

67   Jones, "Cem slams EU," *Cyprus Mail*, March 26, 2002.

Still, most EU officials we interviewed disagreed and claimed that Turkish Cyprus was the problem and that Clerides, in fact, was compromising at the time. It seems clear to us that the EU was taking this view because the alternative would have been to admit a disaster. One senior EU member told us off the record that it would have been "very difficult" for the EU if several of its members came around to Denktaş's position while Clerides stood in its way. Any move to blame the Greek-Cypriots for a breakdown in talks who have put EU enlargement in jeopardy from a virtually certain Greek veto. Thus, Brussels kept insisting that Clerides was compromising even as he was backtracking on elements that had previously been put on the table.

We do share the view that Clerides personally would have liked to have gone down in history as the man who reunited Cyprus, and that he was uniquely positioned to pull off a deal. As one EU observer noted: "Clerides is the wise old bird. No one in the Greek-Cypriot political scene comes close to Mr. Clerides in being able to sell a solution to the Greek-Cypriot people. No one else has the stature. Even his opponents trust his patriotism and good sense." But the EU had made it far more difficult for him to compromise and sell a deal to his fellow Greek-Cypriots. It kept insisting that Clerides was bending over backwards to accommodate the other side, which made little sense when the EU had decided an agreement wasn't necessary to approve Cyprus's membership. Clerides supposed generosity (not evident behind closed doors) gave ammunition to his opponents who rightfully asked why they should compromise when they were in a much more powerful position than Turkish-Cypriots.

Once again, there were many who warned the EU that it was making a mistake. A US special coordinator for Cyprus told a committee of the US House of Representatives in mid-2001, "The British negotiator for EU entry for Cyprus often talks of a train wreck waiting to happen. We believe he is correct. This is the train wreck ready to happen. It could happen in 2002. It could happen in 2003. It could happen sometime thereafter."[68]

A senior EU official told the *Economist*, "it would be a nightmare if the Greek-Cypriots get in on their own."[69]

Ergun Olgun warned that the division of the island would "become permanent, and the political and economic chasm between the two sides will be impossible to bridge"[70] if Cyprus joined the EU divided.

Mustapha Akinci, who was then main opposition leader and later TRNC president, said, "if Cyprus is let into the EU without a settlement, Turkey will integrate us further, even more Turkish settlers will come."[71]

The Cyprus-born philosopher Zenon Stavrinides added: "If the Republic of Cyprus joins the EU without a settlement, the TRNC will become to all intents and purposes a province of Turkey."[72]

68   Hearing before the Subcommittee on Europe of the Committee on International Relations of the US House of Representatives, *US policy in the Eastern Mediterranean*, Washington, June 13,2001,70.

69   "The Cyprus Conundrum," *Economist*, February 22, 2001.

70   Laurent Zecchini, "la Turquie joue a Chypre l'avenir de ses relations avec l'UE," *Le Monde*, March 5, 2002,7.

71   Helena Smith, "A Divided Island in Brussels' embrace," *The Guardian*, November 29, 2001.

72   Zenon Stavrinides, "Is a compromise settlement in Cyprus still possible?," *The Cyprus Review* 11, no. 1 (2000),1.

Admitting a divided Cyprus into the EU essentially achieved *eno-sis*, which thus gave the Greek-Cypriots their maximalist aspirations, although Makarios clearly wanted the whole, not just part, of the island. The risk of this outcome was that the Turkish counter to this *enosis* would be *taksim*, and Turkey did threaten to annex Turkish Cyrpus outright, a move that would have destabilized the entire region.

* * *

This first negative outcome, failure to bring peace to Cyprus, was overshadowed by the second outcome of the EU's handling of this file. The isolation of Turkey was a disaster of the first order. Turkey is at the strategic crossroads of virtually every issue facing the world today. It is a military power and, especially after 9/11, a vital partner for the security of the western world. It is one of the EU's important trading partners, dwarfing Cyprus by comparison. It is a rising power on the energy scene by virtue of its domestic production and pipelines. "Europe really should not turn its back on Turkey," one Turkish diplomat told us. "It is a large country with a powerful military and it would seem to not be in Europe's interest to have Turkey oriented against Europe. This is especially true as Europe and the US compete for influence in the region and as their foreign policies diverge."

Proving that a secular and Muslim nation could thrive and build a democratic state should have been one of the EU's highest strategic priorities. Aligned with that objective, the EU should have been trying to convince the Muslim world that there was no "us against them." Yet one of the unfortunate outcomes of the EU's handling of Cyprus was that the Turks were increasingly frustrated and distrustful of the EU.

Since Ataturk, Turkey's priority and obsession has been westerniza-tion. During the Cold War, that meant membership in Nato. Since the early 2000s, membership in the EU has been the central plank of Turkish foreign policy. The Turkish people were clearly behind this initiative. A 2002 CNN poll showed that 76.5 percent supported and only 22 percent opposed EU membership. Unfortunately, when asked if Turkey would ever be accepted by the EU, 45 percent of the Turkish population said that it would not, and they may be right, Eurobarometer polls from that time showed that 45 percent of Europeans were against Turkey joining the EU while only 30 percent were in favour of it becoming a member. An EU bureaucrat shared the results of an even more damning poll by European MP Pervenche Beres of France, which showed 74 percent of Europeans were against Turkey being admitted to the EU. The Turks desperately wanted into Europe, but Europeans did not reciprocate.

Rather, Europe seemed to hope that Turkey would just go away. As the *Economist* noted in late 2001:

Turkey has worked to join for the best part of four decades. It began building economic ties with the EU's predecessors in 1963. Ten years later it signed a treaty to phase in a customs union, which was eventually completed in 1995. It lodged an application for full membership thirteen years ago. Yet the EU did not get around to accepting Turkey as a candidate until last December.[73]

73 "Why are we waiting'" *Economist,* June 8, 2002.

The European attitudes are unfortunate. While we don't always share the politics of our fellow countryman, former press baron Conrad Black, in this case we completely agree:

> The European practice of embracing the Turks whenever they need an ally in the Middle East and spurning them as a rabble of Islamic migrants whenever they seek a closer association with Europe will lead to disaster. Europe's insane mistreatment of the Middle East's most important country, in which the leading European powers hide behind the Greeks, is in vivid contrast to the whole-hearted generosity of the American and Canadian extension of their free trade agreement to Mexico.[74]

Comments by Enlargement Commissioner Verheugen are an example of this mistreatment and how it undermines Turkey-EU relations. In March 2002, he saw fit to castigate Turkey at a speaking engagement in Athens: "If Turkey carries on threatening Cyprus after its accession, then its own accession process will be cancelled. Turkey is very well aware that it cannot possibly annex part of a country that is a member of the EU."[75] Responding to Verheugen's speech a Turkish reporter stated:

> The fact that people such as Gunter Verheugen are making negative statements that further complicate the Cyprus issue

---

74   Preston, "Tragedy of two races," *The Guardian*, October 26, 1998.
75   Melina Demetriou, "Verheugen: Turkey can forget EU if it annexes the North," *Cyprus Mail*, March 23, 2002.

by antagonizing the Turks . . . hurt the Turkish people and give credence to claims that the EU has ulterior motives . . . Some EU officials should realize that their negative attitudes are only hurting the cause of democracy in Turkey and delaying reform.[76]

The common perception among Turks is that Europe sees no place for a Muslim Turkey within its community. Political elites in Turkey have tended to view EU attitudes as expressions of racism and exclusionism. The decision to exclude Turkey from the accession process confirmed many views in Turkey on European prejudiced attitudes towards Muslim Turkey. Similar assessments have been made well beyond Turkey. "The European powers make it clear that they do not want a Muslim state, Turkey, in the European Union,"[77] writes Samuel Huntington. *The Economist* adds that most observers believe Greece has "stirred the latent anti-Muslim sentiment of its partners to block Turkey's accession. How else, Turks ask, could all the other candidate countries, some of which have little to recommend them, have jumped the queue to end up ahead of their own."[78]

One senior EU official countered this claim and defended Europe's openness. "Islam is the second religion of the EU. This is not a Christian club. Other Islamic nations will want to join in the future." This may be true but the fact remains that the EU is a

76   Ilnur Covik, " Time to make a Decision," *Turkish Daily News*, March 29, 2002.
77   Samuel Huntington, *Clash of Civilizations* (New York: Touchstone, 1996), 126.
78   "Why are we waiting," *Economist*, June 8, 2002.

Christian club. Morocco's application was rejected on "the grounds that Morocco is not a European country."[79] Others believed it was because it was Muslim. In the opinion of many Turks, recent moves to prevent Albania from gaining membership reflect the anti-Muslim bias in the EU. Again, from the *Economist*: "the implicit message that a majority-Muslim state is unwelcome in the EU is one that would shape the bloc for far longer. Albania would join Kosovo, Bosnia and Turkey in the club of spurned Muslim countries."[80]

As one senior Turkish diplomat observed, the EU doesn't really want to have a debate on whether or not it is meant to be homogenous: "It could be explosive with serious consequences. The EU is already having an identity crisis with enlargement. Turkey will provoke broader debate on immigration, which would help the far right in Europe."

This may not be a debate that the Europeans want but eventually they do need to answer the question: do they want non-Christian countries to join? Failure to address it is seriously jeopardizing relations with Turkey among other EU neighbours. As Charlotte Bretherton and John Vogler presciently noted more than twenty years ago, the EU's key security challenge is not defence of its territory "but the need to construct a policy towards its 'near abroad' which responds in a sensitive manner to aspirations for inclusion and fears of exclusion."[81]

79 Bretherton, *The European Union*, 155.
80 "Geopolitics starts at home," *Economist,* January 18, 2020 p. 49.
81 Bretherton, The European Union, 198.

CHAPTER 7

The Annan Plan

A S A DIVIDED CYPRUS hurtled towards joining the EU in 2003 and 2004, both the EU and the UN were doing everything possible to reach a solution to division on the island. The last best hope for a deal was the Annan Plan, named after the then-UN Secretary General Kofi Annan. There were many versions of the plan and, initially, there was genuine support from the Greek-Cypriot leadership under President Glafcos Clerides, although it was not always clear how genuine that support was, or if the Greek-Cypriot people were behind their president as he attempted to negotiate a deal.

In *Reunifying Cyprus: The Annan Plan & Beyond*, author Costa Carras notes that in the twelve months after the introduction of the plan in November 2001, a gap opened between what the public was prepared to tolerate and what its leadership thought was acceptable. Clerides accepted US and UK advice "to make immediate concessions on security to the Turkish military, and this not just in the form of a continuation of the Treaty of Guarantee but in the asymmetric offer of total Cypriot demilitarisation, inclusive of [Greek-Cypriot] defences, combined with a continued Turkish military presence."[82]

The early stages of Annan Plan discussions coincided with the period when the Turkish-Cypriots believed they could deny Cyprus its wish to get into the EU. All observers agree that Rauf Denktaş was delaying the negotiations at every turn and seemingly not interested in getting to a reasonable deal. Lord Hannay told us that "Denktaş hated the EU and spent all his time trying to wreck Turkey's application. He wasted all those years when he could have negotiated compromises with Clerides. Had he done so the EU would have put pressure on the Greek-Cypriots to compromise as well."

The situation took a turn for the worse in February 2002 when Clerides lost the Greek-Cypriot presidential election to Tassos Papadopoulos. Those hoping for a solution to the Cyprus problem could not have landed on a worse Greek-Cypriot leader. There was already little incentive for the Greek-Cypriot side to compromise, as they by now were guaranteed entry into the EU. Papadopoulos, a hawk, understood that he had all the leverage, and he intended to use it. When he had been part of the Greek-Cypriot National Council back in 1992, the minutes report him stating categorically: "Greece has the obligation to tell its EEC partners it will not

---

82 Costa Carras, "The International Relations Aspect of the Annan Plan," in Runifying Cyprus The Annan Plan and Beyond, eds. Andrekos Varnava and Hubert Faustmann (London: I.B. Tauris, 2009), 58.

allow any other country to join the EEC if Cyprus is not admitted at the same time."[83]

Papadopoulos always believed that exploitation of the Greek veto over EU enlargement would get Cyprus into the UN and give Greek-Cypriots the upper hand on the island. But he played his cards close to the vest. Ingemar Lindahl, former Swedish ambassador to Cyprus, says that high-ranking Greek-Cypriot politicians told him that meeting with the UN in New York, Papadopoulos "accepted the Annan Plan and only wanted to strengthen its functionality."[84] Later, he deliberately undermined what the Greek-Cypriot National Council had accepted in New York as the roadmap for adoption of the Annan Plan.

The Greek-Cypriot National Council had been naïve to trust Papadopoulos. It is clear from statements dating back to 1992 that he never accepted the basic framework that was being proposed. He declared in the newspaper *Harevgi*, as quoted in former President Vassiliou's book, that it was not "an acceptable or even tolerable basis for carrying out negotiations."[85] Papadopoulos, as we will see, is responsible for the ultimate disaster of Cyprus entering the EU as a divided country.

Meanwhile, across the water in Turkey, certain developments had made a Cyprus deal more likely. In November 2002, Recep Tayyip Erdoğan's Justice and Development Party (AKP) won the

83 George Vassiliou, *From the President's Office* (London: I.B. Tauris, 2010), 149.
84 Ingemar Lindahl, *Notes from the Graveyard of Diplomats* (Limassol, Cyprus: Heterotopia, 2019), 298.
85 Vassiliou, *President's Office*, 173.

election in Turkey. The AKP was keen on joining the EU and more open than its predecessor to a Cyprus solution. This change in leadership would eventually lead to increased pressure on Denktaş to negotiate genuinely. Denktaş did, in fact, apply himself constructively at this stage, but unfortunately his sparring partner was now Papadopoulos, who was only interested in running down the clock until Cyprus could get into the EU with no deal. A successful negotiation requires at least two willing participants.

In New York City in February 2004, Papadopoulos refused to shake the hand of the Turkish-Cypriot negotiator, declined to have any contact with the Turks, and even refused to prioritize his list of demands. This obstructionist behaviour was noticed by observers. "It was clear that Papadopoulos had proven to be an extremely difficult negotiator," wrote Ambassador Lindahl, "a negotiator who didn't want to negotiate."[86]

Despite continued resistance from the Greek Cypriot leaders, a fifth and final version of the Annan Plan was presented in March 2004. This was to be voted on in twin referendums on both sides of the island on April 24, 2004. The UN had led an extensive and comprehensive negotiating effort which included fifty-four meetings during the introductory phase, seventy-two face-to-face meetings between the two sets of negotiators, and more than 150 separate bilateral meetings between UN negotiator Alvaro de Soto and the two leaders. The Annan Plan ran to 192 pages with an additional 250 pages of finalized laws for the new Cyprus. It was

86   Lindahl, *Notes from the Graveyard*, 246.

No separation of church and state: Archbishop Makarios III was the first President of Cyprus after independence in 1960. He changed the constitution, abrogating the rights of Turkish Cypriots.

In 1964, the UN Peacekeeping Force in Cyprus (UNFICYP) was created to quell the interethnic violence on the island. Over the decades, some 35,000 Canadian soldiers have served in Cyprus.

On July 7, 1974, Nicos Sampson declared himself the new President of Cyprus, after Archbishop Makarios was overthrown. The British gave him the nickname "the Executioner of Murder Mile" for his role in violence against British soldiers.

Mustafa Bülent Ecevit was the four-time Prime Minister of Turkey. His tenure included the 1974 Turkish invasion of Cyprus. He is seen here with US President George W. Bush towards the end of his last term in 2002.

A 1980 group photo of Canadian UNFICYP soldiers from Recce Platoon, 3 PPCLI. Co-Author Lawrence Stevenson is in the first row, second from right.

In June 1992, former UN Secretary-General Boutros Boutros Ghali met with Greek Cypriot leader George Vassiliou and Turkish Cypriot leader Rauf Denktas in an attempt at brokering a peace deal.

UN Secretary-General Kofi Annan with Greek Cypriot leader Glafcos Clerides in 2002. Clerides was seen as the prime mover helping get Cyprus into the European Union.

Kofi Annan shakes hands with Papadopoulos and Denkta in February 2004, before peace talks—and the high hopes of the Annan plan—crumbled two months later.

Vladimir Putin's influence in Cyprus is considerable; Russians and Greek Cypriots have been connected by shared faith, more recently by investment. Putin and Greek Cypriot President Nicos Anastasiades have a close working relationship.

Cyprus is home to some of the most beautiful beaches in Europe, and a deal to reunify Cyprus would lead to an incredible boom in tourism on the island.

In October 2020, Erdogan's preferred candidate, Ersin Tatar, won election to the presidency of the TRNC.

The Hala Sultan Mosque and Theological Centre in North Nicosia was funded by Turkey. Opened in 2018, complete with a state-visit by Erdogan, it is now the largest mosque complex in the mostly secular TRNC.

detailed: fourteen technical committees had written 140 draft laws.

Given that the Annan Plan is the closest the Cypriots have come to reconciliation and that the plan would form the basis for any future deal, it is worth pausing over its key elements. Annan proposed a united Cyprus: "an independent state in the form of an undissolvable partnership, with a federal government and two equal constituent states, the Greek-Cypriot State and the Turkish-Cypriot State." This was the bi-zonal, bi-communal federal structure that had formed the basis of all formal negotiations between the two parties going back to the original Makarios-Denktaş talks. Cyprus would be a federal republic loosely based on the Swiss model. The two constituent parts of the country would not be able to leave the federation or join with other countries. Both maximalist positions, *enosis* and *taksim*, were permanently off the table.

As in any federal state, such as exists today in Canada, the federal government would be responsible for certain areas and the constituent states would cover others. The federal government under the Annan Plan would control immigration, foreign policy, and international relations. Most everything else would be the responsibility of the two states. The new Cyprus would have a federal parliament made up of two houses. A lower house (Chamber of Deputies) would have forty-eight members and at least twelve of them had to be Turkish-Cypriots. An upper house (Senate) would also have forty-eight members with an equal number from both ethnic communities. Decisions made by parliament needed a simple majority of both houses. This effectively meant that the

Turkish Cypriot would no longer have the veto given to them in the 1960 constitution—a huge concession—but it also meant that their representation would protect their minority rights.

The executive power would rest with the six voting members of the presidential council. At least two of these six voting members had to come from each of the ethnic communities. Thus the Turkish-Cypriots were sure to have at least two of the six voting members. Decisions were to be made by simple majority but that majority had to include at least one member from each constituent group. The principle was that the Greek-Cypriot majority was recognized but at the same time the Turkish-Cypriot minority was protected. Not equal, but protected, a workable compromise. Under this arrangement, there would again be a need for both communities to compromise in order to govern. The supreme court would resolve disputes between states and between the states and the federal government. The court would have nine members; three Greek-Cypriots, three Turkish-Cypriots, and three non-Cypriot judges who could not be Greek, Turkish, or British.

In terms of territory, the Turkish-Cypriot state would be reduced from the 36 percent that it currently occupies to 28.5 percent of Cyprus land area, and this territorial adjustment would be accomplished over four years. Property was always one of the most complex issues to resolve. Many Greek-Cypriots who had lived in the north pre-1974, and fewer Turkish-Cypriots who had lived in the south, lost their homes as a result of the invasion by Turkey. The Annan Plan offered a combination of compensation, restitution and exchange to address this thorny issue. The Greek-Cypriots who lost territory that was being returned to the Greek-Cypriot state could get their property back. Those not entitled to get their property back in the new north Turkish-Cypriot state would be compensated.

Security and guarantees were a sore point, particularly for the Greek-Cypriots. Under the plan, the three treaties of establishment, guarantee and alliance would remain in force. The three guarantor powers (Greece, Turkey and Britain) would still apply. As part of the plan, Britain would give up almost half of the 98 square miles of Cypriot territory covered by its sovereign base areas. Annan also called for the gradual demilitarization of Cyprus. The Cypriot security forces would be disbanded and both Greece and Turkey could keep up to 6,000 soldiers in Cyprus for seven years. In 2018 (or earlier if Turkey joined the EU) this would be reduced to 3,000 soldiers for each of the Greeks and the Turks. This would subsequently be reduced to 950 Greek and 650 Turkish troops as had been stipulated in the 1960 Treaty of Alliance. The aim was to withdraw eventually all Greek and Turkish soldiers.

The Annan Plan was not perfect, and it certainly did not include everything that either the Greek-Cypriots or the Turkish-Cypriots wanted in a final deal. But it was workable. It built on all the previous negotiations and adhered to the principles of majority rule with significant protections for the Turkish-Cypriot minority. It gave Turkish-Cypriots less power than they had been given at independence in 1960 but it also gave them something they did not have in 1960, which was their own constituent state. It was the "art of the possible," given the realities on the ground. It was the best hope for Cyprus, but it was not about to happen because of the leadership of one person: Tassos Papadopoulos.

The plan could have worked if the Greek-Cypriot public had been convinced of the logic of this deal versus the likely implications of the status quo, but Papadopoulos did everything in his power to undercut the Annan Plan in the eyes of the Greek-Cypriot public. His prime minister, Marcus Kyprianou, presented a report in December 2003 on the economic consequences of the plan. It predicted dire consequences for the Greek-Cypriots. As Ambassador Lindahl rightly claims: "It is difficult not to suspect that this report was commissioned by Papadopoulos as a means of negatively influencing the Greek-Cypriots against the [Annan] plan. Since he has no other choice than commit himself politically to it, he resorts to non-political ways to undermine it."[87]

As soon as the final version of the Annan Plan was tabled, Papadopoulos launched his full assault to ensure that Greek Cypriots would vote against it. As Lord Hannay says:

> In the south, the rejectionists had a field day. When Papadopoulos did declare his hand, in a lengthy, rambling and emotional television presentation, he did not confine himself to the details of the [plan] but rather launched a root-and-branch onslaught on the fundamentals of the UN's approach. . . . He thus disposed of any illusion that he might in fact have been negotiating in good faith up to the last moment.[88]

As Papadopoulos said in his address, the Greek-Cypriot people had to reject the Annan Plan to save the republic, "the only foothold of

---

87 Lindahl, *Notes from Graveyard*, 195.
88 Hannay, *Cyprus Search for Solution*, 245.

our people and the guarantee of our historic character." He went on to say, "I was given an internationally recognized state and I am not going to give back a community."[89]

The rejectionists branded peace negotiators and pro-reunification activists as traitors and took some to court. Papadopoulos was largely backed by the media in the south; the Greek Orthodox Church also strongly backed the "no" vote. The church has consistently been against any deal to reunite the island under any terms that might be acceptable to the Turkish-Cypriots. At least they have been consistent. Years earlier when the UN Set of Ideas had been presented, former Cypriot president Vassiliou reported, "The Archbishop [Chrysostomos] went so far as to send a letter to Karmanlis [four-time prime minister and two-time president of Greece] accusing us [Vassiliou's government] of treason."[90] Unlike Papadopoulos, who hid his cards until the last minute and gamed the system and the EU, the church was always forthright about being against any deal, including the Annan Plan.

The scaremongering continued. "Pensioners have been told that the UN Plan might deprive them of their pension, police and National Guard officers that they might lose their jobs and civil servants that they would face pay reductions," writes Ambassador Lindhal. "The Holy Synod . . . has used the church services to admonish the faithful to defend the land against the godless foreigners."[91]

---

89 Lindahl, *Notes from Graveyard*, 252-53.
90 Vassiliou, *President's Office*, 172.
91 Lindahl, *Notes from Graveyard*, 258.

In a slap to the UN and the EU, the Greek-Cypriot government censored messages from both institutions so that the Greek-Cypriots would not hear the case to vote "yes." Additionally, Papadopoulos accused his opponents of having been bought off with US and UN funds.[92] "We do think that there was a lot of manipulation by the Greek Cypriot leaders in the run up to the election," said US state department spokesman Richard Boucher. "The outcome was regrettable but not surprising given these actions."[93]

The final nail in the coffin for the Annan Plan was driven as Papadopoulos complained about a lack of safeguards and guarantees for the implementation of the plan. The US and UK presented a draft UN Security Council resolution to address this concern. Again, as Lord Hannay explains: "The Security Council would have endorsed the whole package and committed itself to its prescribed role in its implementation had there not been a disgraceful last-minute veto by the Russian Federation, acting at the behest of Papadopolous, who then argued in the closing days of the campaign that it was impossible to have confidence in the settlement because it had not been endorsed by the Security Council."[94] Ambassador Lindahl detailed in his memoirs how Greek-Cypriot Foreign Minister Iacovou flew to Moscow to convince Russia to veto the

---

92   Yiannis Laouris, Marios Michaelides and Romina Laouris, "A Systematic Evaluation of the State of Affairs following the Negative Outcome of the Referendum in Cyprus using the Structured Dialogic Design Process," paper at *researchgate.net*, February 2009, 59.

93   "The US accuses Greek Cypriot Leaders of Derailing Unification Vote," *New York Times*, April 27, 2004.

94   Hannay, *Cyprus Search for Solution*, 244.

resolution written to provide Greek-Cypriots the safeguards they said they so desperately needed.[95] The Russians obliged.

On April 24, 2004, Cypriots voted on the Annan Plan. Turkish-Cypriots approved it with a solid 65 percent in favour. The Greek-Cypriots rejected it with close to 76 percent against. The greatest opportunity for a Cypriot resolution had gone to waste. The rejectionists celebrated and a week later, on May 1, 2004, Cyprus entered the EU with only the Greek-Cypriots enjoying the benefits of membership.

Many Greek-Cypriots rejoiced in this outcome. "With their vote in 2004," wrote Costa Carras, "the Greek-Cypriots stood up for the principle of justice and international law, thus again opening the way to a genuine and lasting peace for Cyprus."[96] Canan Balkir and Galip Yalman explained that "the Greek-Cypriots now see EU membership as an alternative to a settlement and as a means to negate the Turkish military guarantee and exert pressure to deliver the Turkish-Cypriots into their hands."[97] This was telegraphed in advance of the vote. Many Greek-Cypriots arguing against the Annan Plan had ventured that on entering the EU, "Cyprus would be in the strongest negotiating position since 1974, and that the application of EU laws and regulations will protect more effectively the rights of all Cypriots."[98]

---

95 Lindahl, *Notes from Graveyard*, 265.
96 Carras, "International Relations Aspect of Annan Plan," 65.
97 Canan Balkir and Galip Yalman, "Economics and the politicization of civil society: the Turkish-Cypriot case," in *Cyprus a conflict at the crossroads,* eds. Thomas Diez and Nathalie Tocci (Manchester: Manchester University Press, 2009), 57.
98 Christophoros Christophorou and Craig Webster, "Greek Cypriots, Turkish

This may have been the sentiment of the rejectionists in 2004, but here we are eighteen years later and we are certainly no closer to "lasting peace". Greek-Cypriots promised their electorate a better deal with Turkish-Cypriots once they had been admitted to the EU. That better deal is nowhere to be seen. As with the Brexiteers, many false promises were made to sway "no" voters. Papadapolous sold a mirage and fooled everyone, including his own citizens, the EU, and the UN.

Papadopoulos's performance was predictable. Back in July 1992, he was quoted in *Elephtherotypia* saying that "there is no space either in the small strip of our sacred land or in the wide horizons of our national conscience for even an inch of national land to be granted to the Turkish invader and thus confirm partition with our own signature."[99] This was never going to be the man to lead the Greek-Cypriots to a compromise deal with Turkish-Cypriots. Ambassador Lindahl quotes former President Clerides as saying of Papadopoulos, "A leopard will not change his spots."[100]

The Greek-Cypriot rejection of the plan was viewed with dismay in the TRNC, Washington, London, New York, and Brussels. It especially stung the EU and the UN. As Alvaro de Soto, the UN's special advisor on Cyprus, wrote in his report to the Secretary General: "The decision of the Greek-Cypriots is a major setback. If they remain willing to resolve the Cyprus problem through a

Cyriots and the Future: The Day after the Referendum," a *Development Associates Occasional Paper in Democracy and Governance*, November 16th, 2004,12.
99 Vassiliou, *President's Office*, 196.
100 Lindahl, *Notes from Graveyard*, 189.

bi-communal, bi-zonal federation, this needs to be demonstrated."[101] The world is still waiting for such a demonstration.

The EU reaction was immediate and extremely negative. It had been played by the Greek-Cypriots, as Verheugen, the EU enlargement commissioner, admitted: "I will be very undiplomatic now in saying that I personally feel that I have been cheated by the Republic of Cyprus." [102] He repeated this charge in a speech to the European Parliament in Strasbourg in late April 2004, accusing the Greek-Cypriots of cheating their way into the EU. "The decision in 1999 not to make a solution to the Cyprus conflict a prerequisite for Cyprus accession to the EU was on the understanding that the government of Cyprus would do everything in its power to resolve the problem." [103]

That the EU had been played by the Greek-Cypriots was obvious to many others. When Greek-Cypriot Foreign Minister Iacovou went to the EU after the referendum to soothe ruffled feathers, he was treated to a verbal lashing from numerous members. Carl Hamilton, Sweden's vice-chair of EU affairs, told Iacovou that "you cheated yourself into the EU by rejecting the EU Plan when you knew that the entry of Cyprus would no longer be stopped."[104] Gunilla Carlsson, chair of the EU foreign relations committee, told Iacovou that he "deliberately brought a frozen conflict into

101 Lindahl, *Notes from Graveyard*, 308.
102 Chris Patten, EU Commissioner for External Relations, "Being badly let down'" *www.hri.org*, 100.
103 Lindahl, *Notes from Graveyard*, 261.
104 Lindahl, *Notes from Graveyard*, 286.

the EU."[105] She told Iacovou that the Greek-Cypriots had better work on a new referendum soon, and this time support it. Unfortunately, that was not going to happen.

Iacovou and the Greek-Cypriots could easily bear the tongue-lashings. They had won. They were in the EU and from that position, their hand was stronger, or at least they thought so at the time. They believed they could force both the Turkish-Cypriots and Turkey itself, given the latter's hope to enter the EU, to accept terms more favorable to the Greek-Cypriots than those offered in the Annan Plan.

The only seemingly good news for the Turkish-Cypriots from the overwhelming Greek-Cypriot rejection of the referendum was that their isolation was now going to end. Both the EU and the UN supported ending the isolation of Northern Cyprus due to their acceptance of the compromises in the Annan Plan. Kofi Annan, the UN secretary general himself, stated in this report to the UN Security Council on May 28, 2004: "I would hope [members of the Security Council] can give a strong lead to all states to cooperate both bilaterally and in International bodies to eliminate unnecessary restrictions and barriers that have the effect of isolating the Turkish-Cypriots and impeding their development."[106]

EU Commissioner Verheugen had said before the vote that if the Greek-Cypriots were to vote no, the EU would end the economic isolation of Turkish Cyprus. This promise was repeated in

105 Lindahl, *Notes from Graveyard*, 286.
106 Mustafa Ergun Olgun, "one final chance for Federalism," in *Resolving Cyprus*, ed. James Ker-Lindsay (London: I.B. Tauris, 2015), 212.

other EU statements. It was not kept as the Greek-Cypriots, with their seat in the EU, blocked support for the Turkish-Cypriots at every turn. Their economic isolation continued. As the former Turkish-Cypriot minister of foreign affairs and Turkish-Cypriot negotiator Ozdil Nami told us when we met him in the summer of 2019, "We were cheated by Verheugen and the EU. They said that a country with internal borders would not be allowed in."

The rejection of the Annan Plan was a bitter pill for the Turkish-Cypriots. As Stavrinides writes in *Reunifying Cyprus*, "the Turkish-Cypriots felt that by rejecting the Annan Plan the Greek-Cypriots had rejected them . . . that means that they have transformed a political action by the Greek-Cypriot community as a hostile personal act that is directed towards them."[107] These scars will not easily heal, and it is now possible that reconciliation is a dead letter.

The EU clearly misplayed its hand, giving up its leverage over the Greek-Cypriots by effectively guaranteed them admission in Helsinki. As Christian Danielsson, the chef de cabinet to the EU's Verhaegen, confessed to Ambassador Lindahl: "[Verhaegen] regretted that there had not been a stronger clause . . . about the entry of a reunited Cyprus into the EU. Now it was too late to stop the train."[108]

We contend that the Greek-Cypriots blew the chance, as well. They imagined that they had played a clever hand but they have

---

107 Panicos Stavrinides, "A Psychological Analysis of the Greek Cypriot 'No'," in *Reunifying Cyprus The Annan Plan and Beyond*, eds. Andrekos Varnava and Hubert Faustmann (London: I.B. Tauris, 2009), 213-14.
108 Lindahl, *Notes from Graveyard*, 256.

lost in the long-term. The "no" vote in 2004, writes Lord Hannay, was "a strategic error. Yet again, as in the 1963, and 1974, they opted for a narrow, crabbed vision of the future, dictated more by emotional memories of the past than by a rational view of the future. They will now have to live with the consequences of that decision."[109] Papadopoulos achieved his aim in getting Cyprus into the EU without having to compromise with the Turkish-Cypriots, but he missed a once-in-a-lifetime opportunity, with a willing negotiator on the Turkish-Cypriot side of the table, and another in Ankara, to get a united Cyprus. At a time when the Greek-Cypriots needed a leader like Vassiliou or Clerides, they were led by a crabbed, myopic tactician. It is cold comfort that Papadopoulos lost his next election; contrary to his assumption that the Turkish-Cypriots would give him all he wanted once Cyprus was in the EU, no such outcome was forthcoming.

* * *

Clearly the Greek-Cypriot leadership deserves the lion's share of blame for the failure of the Annan Plan. It is also true, as we have pointed out in earlier chapters, that the EU played its hand poorly. But the fact remains that over three in four Greek-Cypriot citizens voted against the plan. This was not a razor-thin, Brexit-like vote. Given that any future resolution will use the Annan Plan as a foundation, it is worth asking why the Greek-Cypriots voted so

109 Hannay, *Cyprus*, 245-46

overwhelmingly against it. Kaymak, Lordos, and Tocci surveyed a thousand Cypriots in May 2008 to explore this question. As shown below, the survey found that 64 percent of Greek-Cypriots found the Annan Plan "unacceptable" and a further 24 percent found the plan only "tolerable." Only 12 percent of Greek-Cypriots found it "satisfactory or highly desirable." By contrast, 44 percent of Turkish-Cypriots found the plan "unacceptable" and 30 percent found it "satisfactory or highly desirable."

Yet when asked if they supported a bi-zonal, bi-communal (BZBC) federation with political equality, a strong majority of both communities were in favour.

If you combine the 34 percent of Greek-Cypriots who said such a BZBC federation was highly desirable with the 29 percent who said it was satisfactory, fully 63 percent supported the concept. Yet a bi-zonal, bi-communal federation with political equality is exactly what the Annan Plan proposed. How could 64 percent of Greek-Cypriots be against the Annan Plan (and 76 percent voted against the plan in the 2004 referendum) while 63 percent say that they are fine with a BZBC federation with political equality? The reason is that the very concept of a BZBC federation with political equality is Delphic. It is what you want it to be. Each side sees it differently and supports it in principle but the Greek-Cypriots do not support it once the details are fleshed out, as they were in the Annan Plan.

Kaymak, Lordos, and Tocci found five main areas of disagreement between the two sides with regard to the Annan Plan. The only item both favoured was that "each community should have the right to block any decision or legislation of the federal government that it considers to be incompatible with its own communal interests." Some 41 percent of Greek Cypriots said that this was "essential or satisfactory" while fewer (38 percent) said it was "unacceptable or tolerable." While the Greek-Cypriots registered this slight net agreement with the statement, 72 percent of Turkish-Cypriots found it "essential or satisfactory."

On the four other points, the two sides are miles apart, with one party in favour and the other firmly opposed.

There is no common ground on the issue of resolving the property issue through restitution. There is a wide difference on the return of settlers in the TRNC to Turkey, another on whether or not the ethnic groups should stay primarily in their own states, and another with respect to demilitarization.

The Annan Plan tried to weave a path through these issues that would have been acceptable to the majority in both ethnic groups. The polling above suggests that it was fortunate to have got as far as it did. It will be very difficult to thread this needle in the future. Any adjustments to the Annan Plan to make it more acceptable to the Greek-Cypriot community will certainly be resisted by the Turkish-Cypriots, and could undermine their support for it, the one positive outcome of 2004.

CHAPTER 8

Debunking Myths about Cyprus

AS MENTIONED EARLIER, an understanding of the real history of Cyprus is vital to arriving at a fair and lasting solution to its problems. Standing in the way of that understanding are four myths about Cyprus which most casual observers accept at face value:

Myth #1: The Turkish and Greek Cypriots have previously lived happily together and can easily do so again.

Myth #2: There were incidents of violence but both communities were responsible, and the worst offenders were the Greeks, particularly the right-wing military junta.

Myth #3: The Turks invaded Cyprus with no right to do so and they, and they alone, have been responsible for the problems on the island today.

Myth #4: Partition of the island is an unworkable solution that was dreamed up by Turkey and has never been considered by the international community.

Listen to most US, UN and EU diplomats and you quickly find a near universal acceptance of these four myths. They are primary reasons why the international community has made so little progress in Cyprus. Let us examine each myth in turn.

Myth #1: The Turkish and Greek Cypriots have previously lived happily together and can easily do so again.

Cypriot Ambassador to the EU Theophilos Theophilou told us in an interview in Brussels in 2002 that the problem in Cyprus before 1974 was "outside influences. [Turkey's] intervention and outright invasion are what caused the problems. We lived together for centuries in the same neighbourhoods with no problems whatsoever."

International optimists point to the village of Pyla in the UN buffer zone where Greek-Cypriots and Turkish-Cypriots have supposedly lived happily together to paint a vivid portrait of what could be on the whole island. But as Chris Morris reported in the *Guardian*: "Greeks never visit the Turkish coffee houses, and the Turks don't go to the Greek restaurants a few yards across the square."[110] We visited Pyla in the summer of 2019 and found things exactly as described by Morris. The two sides live together

110 Chris Morris, "Divided Village damps hope for Cyprus Unity," *The Guardian*, July 1, 2000.

but don't like each other and rarely mix, which is basically a prescription for the whole island.

Others point to the fact that the two communities today live side-by-side in several of the world's metropoli. But as Rauf Denktaş told us, "People say that Greeks and Turks live happily together in London or New York, but there you do not have one trying to impose his will on the other."

The reality is that Turkish-Cypriots and Greek-Cypriots have never lived happily together. For most of modern history, they were forced to live on the same island by an outside power, first the Ottomans, and then the British. This external power controlled the locals and the two sides had no choice but to get along. Otherwise, they were separate and distinct at all times. Under the Ottomans, inter-marriage was considered as bad as incest. The only experience of living together without an external controlling power lasted a brief three years, in the early 1960s. The period 1963-74 was a disaster for the Turkish-Cypriot minority. It is safe to say that most Greek-Cypriots view this period as one of "general harmony with a few incidents caused by extremists on both sides," as one diplomat told us. Another observer noted: "The majority of Greek Cypriots do not think very hard about any injustice, indignities, and deprivations that the Turkish-Cypriots may have suffered either in the years before 1974 or since." The Turks, however, don't forget the slights they have suffered as second-class citizens in their own country. As Denktaş reminisced in 2002:

> We went to a joint school. The Greek-Cypriots talk about how we got along when we lived together, but we Turkish-Cypriots

were second class citizens. It was like being under Hitler where they [the Greek-Cypriots] were the masters. Your school friend would call you by saying "Hey Mad Turk" or "Hey Dirty Turk come here."

Of course, the indignity of being called a "mad turk" might seem insignificant when compared to the second myth of Cypriot history.

Myth #2: There were incidents of violence but both communities were responsible and the worst offenders were the Greeks, particularly the right-wing military junta and the Greek Cypriot EOKA.

The official guidebook published by the government of Cyprus in 2000 has this to say about the trouble in 1963: "When in 1963 the President of the Republic proposed some amendments to facilitate the functioning of the state, the Turkish community responded with rebellion (December 1964), the Turkish Ministers withdrew from the Cabinet and the Turkish Public Servants ceased attending their offices."[111]

It is so unbelievable as to be laughable. One can perhaps forgive the Greek-Cypriots their propaganda machine, but what is not so forgivable is that the international community has generally and uncritically accepted this version of events. In its summary of the history of the island, the European Union has this to say on its website in 2002:

111 *Cyprus General Tourist Information Handbook*, Nicosia, 2000, 25.

In 1960, Cyprus became an independent state. The agreements provided for a division of power along communal lines. This played into the hands of nationalism. Politicians, lacking experience of democratic culture, made little efforts to establish consensus. The outcome was a political crisis, which spilled over into fighting on the streets in 1963. Finally, the Turkish Cypriots withdrew from the common institutions in 1964. The United Nations sent forces—UNFICYP—to the island for the first time, which are still there.[112]

This is a strange and objectionable view of history. It suggests the two parties to the dispute are equally to blame when the so-called political crisis was caused by Greek-Cypriot leaders unilaterally changing the constitution to deprive Turkish-Cypriots of the rights they were given at independence. And a dispute that "spilled over into fighting on the streets in 1963" is a strange euphemism for ethnic-cleansing, which the EU rightly did not accept later in Bosnia.

The ethnic cleansing was very much one-sided and very much initiated by Greek-Cypriots, not Greeks. As international lawyer and former British MP Michael Stephen points out:

The international community has been, and still is, willing to overlook a systematic attempt to genocide by the Greek-Cypriots in 1963, and again in 1964, 1967, and 1974, and

112 "Relations with Cyprus," *Europa.eu.int*, 4.

the destruction by the Greek-Cypriots in 1963 of the republic, which was established by the 1960 Constitution and guaranteed by international treaty.[113]

As Christopher Hitchens recounts:

> I have visited the mass graves of Alloa and Maratha and Sandallaris, three little villages just outside the city of Famagusta, where hundreds of Turkish-Cypriot civilian corpses were dug up like refuse in the ghastly summer of 1974. And I have toured the burned-out ruin of Omorphita, a Turkish-Cypriot suburb that was devastated by Nicos Sampson's gang of terrorists in 1963. I have no difficulty in sympathizing with Turkish-Cypriot fears, and I do not believe that they have been manufactured out of thin air.[114]

Today, Greek-Cypriots love to proclaim that all the island's problems started in 1974 and that this violence was caused by Greeks and not Greek-Cypriots. This is simply inaccurate. The persecution of Turkish-Cypriots in 1963-64 and 1967, the efforts of Greek-Cypriot to eliminate their neighbours, was far worse than anything to happen subsequently. Makarios declared in 1970, "I have always been in favor of *enosis*,"[115] and he was still willing to commit genocide to get it. He is still revered as a hero in Cyprus today with the main

---

113 Stephen, *Perceptions*, 1.
114 Hitchens, *Hostage to History*, 40.
115 Christopher de Bellaigue, "Conciliation in Cyprus," *Washington Quarterly* (Spring 1999), 187.

boulevard in Nicosia named after him. Had he committed his acts today rather than in the 1960s, he would be charged with war crimes much like Slobodan Milosevic. The facts are the same; only the tolerance of the international community has changed.

It is no wonder that Denktaş insisted to us, correctly, in 2002: "For Greek-Cypriots, history started in 1974. For us it started on December 21, 1963 with the break-up of the partnership."

Myth #3: The Turks invaded without any right to do so and they, and they alone, have been responsible for the problems of Cyprus today.

We have already treated the legality of the Turkish action and it seems clear that phase one of the intervention was legal and phase two may have been depending on which lawyer is talking and who pays for his or her opinion. But we do want to deal with the international community's perception that the Turkish-Cypriots are the guilty party. As we have seen, the true picture is as follows:

- The Greek-Cypriots unilaterally and illegally tore up the 1960 constitution
- The Greek-Cypriots engaged in ethnic cleansing in 1963 and again in 1967
- The Greek-Cypriot mother country, Greece, precipitated the 1974 crisis by overthrowing the government of Cyprus and pushing *enosis* in clear violation of the 1960 agreements
- Both sides have frustrated UN negotiations over the past twenty years, although the Greek-Cypriots have been the more intransigent party, particularly with regard to the Annan Plan.

As early as 1964, the international community was blaming the Turks, and only a few international observers were willing to push back on this narrative. Patrick Dean of the British delegation in New York, wrote a letter dated August 12, 1964 in which he stated:

> It is curious and sometimes very frustrating to sit in the Security Council and walk around the UN and have to listen to all the stuff about the wickedness of the Turks and their threats of invasion, when I and all my staff know very well what the real state of affairs is, and how much Makarios and company are to blame.[116]

This same bias has been evident in the US, as was noted by Dan Burton, Republican congressman from Indiana, at a June 2001 US House of Representatives subcommittee hearing:

> In the past, the Congress has not dealt with Cyprus issues in an even-handed manner. Hearings have been less concerned about finding a balanced, long-term political solution and more concerned about denouncing Turkish-Cypriots, denouncing Rauf Denktaş, and pressuring Turkey to stop providing security for Turkish-Cypriots on the northern part of Cyprus. . . . I want to emphasize that the division of Cyprus was not caused by Turkey or the Turkish-Cypriots, it was caused by Greece and Greek-Cypriots. Prior to the Turkish intervention on Cyprus in 1974, Turkish-Cypriots had been forcibly expelled from their

---

116 Salahi Sonyel, "New Light on the Genesis of the Conflict," in *Cyprus The Need for New Perspectives*,34.

own government, and Turkish-Cypriots were being slaughtered in tremendous numbers. It was to save lives and protect Turkish-Cypriots from further slaughter that the Turkish military intervened in Cyprus.[117]

These comments by Dean and Burton have given the international community opportunity to reconsider its position on Cyprus and appreciate that while both parties contributed to the problem, an objective reading of the facts shows Turkey and the Turkish-Cypriots to be the less guilty party. US Ambassador to Cyprus John Koenig got into hot water when he spoke the truth in a speech at the University of Cyprus in May 2015 saying that "I do not regard the Cyprus problem as a problem of invasion and occupation." Indeed the Cyprus problem did not start in 1974.

Myth #4: Partition of the island is an unworkable solution that was dreamed up by Turkey and has ever been considered by the international community.

The de facto partition in Cyprus today is a result of the Turkish invasion of 1974, after all of its other options had failed. Ever since, the Turkish-Cypriot half of the island has not been recognized internationally, and the international community will not consider partition. Indeed, partition is never discussed as an option except

---

117 Hearing before the Subcommittee on Europe of the Committee on International Relations of the US House of Representatives, *US Policy in the Eastern Mediterranean*, Washington, June 13, 2001,5.

in Ankara and Northern Cyprus. But, as we have already shown, both the British (in the 1950s) and the US (in the 1960s and 70s) believed partition of the island to be a viable road to peace. Denktaş quotes Kissinger as saying "that in ethnic conflict, settlement is never going back to the old days. Either one side silences the other or there is division." Kissinger was clearly in favour of partition. On August 13th, 1974, which was the day before the second phase of the Turkish invasion, Kissinger met with President Ford (who had been in office for 4 days) and National Security Advisor Brent Scowcroft in the Oval Office and pointed out the "There is no reason why the Turks should not have one-third of Cyprus."[118]

De facto partition has hardly been the worst thing to happen to Cyprus. As Andrew Mango says:

> The absence of bloodshed in Cyprus, achieved since 1974, is a boon to be treasured. There has been no bloodshed because the island's inhabitants are secure in their lives, homes and property, and because men of violence have been kept apart. Any settlement, which jeopardizes this security, would lead to a renewal of intercommunal violence . . . People say "apply to Cyprus EU rules on freedom of movement, freedom of settlement, etc." without thinking what would follow. But the consequences are easy to predict."[119]

---

118 *Fordlibrarymuseum.gov*/library/document/0314/1552748.pdf
119 Ergun Olgun, "Confederation: The Last Chance for Establishing a New Partnership in Cyprus,"in *Perceptions*, Volume VI, no. 1 (Marchn -May 2001.

A unitary state was tried in Cyprus in 1960, and within three short years it failed miserably. If anything, one can hypothesize that a single Cyprus state might fare worse today than it did in then. At a 1997 conference in Cyprus, criminologist Don Lindley mused that, "any solution that forces the two sides to live and govern together when they do not appear to be ready would cause a disaster."[120]

A March 2000 poll revealed the attitudes of Greek and Turkish Cypriots to one another.[121] Three out of four Greek-Cypriots said they would not accept a family member marrying a Turkish-Cypriot. Four out of five said that even with a solution they would not live in the Turkish-Cypriot part of Cyprus and "between 30 percent and 40 percent were against working in the same place as a Turkish-Cypriot, living in a mixed village, or allowing their children to attend the same schools as Turkish-Cypriot children." As one senior EU diplomat told us, "If we have a settlement now it will be a settlement founded on distrust."

Nanette Neuwahl believes there is a natural tendency in federated states for minority communities separated from the majority by cultural, religious, or linguistic factors "to want to break loose, as is the case with Quebec in Canada."[122] We agree with her general

---

120 Dan Lindley, "UNFICYP and a Cyprus Solution: A Strategic Assessment," *A Security Studies Working Paper for MIT*, Inter College Conference, South Cyprus, May, 1997, 1-11.

121 Erol Kaymak, Alexandros Lordos and Nathalie Tocci, *Building Confidence in Peace* (Brussels: Centre for European Policy Studies, 2009),9.

122 Nanette Neuwahl, "Cyprus: Which Way? – In Pursuit of a Confederal Solution in Europe," *Harvard Law School Jean Monnet Working Paper 4*, April, 2000, 8.

point but would suggest that Cyprus is far more challenging than the situation in Canada and Quebec, for three reasons. First, there exists a history of conflict and genocide in Cyprus, which has never been the case in Quebec. Second, there is a dramatic economic disparity between Turkish and Greek Cyprus whereas Quebec's economic income is similar to that of the rest of Canada. Finally, the Turkish-Cypriots have been and are still regarded as lesser beings by the Greek-Cypriots and this is clearly not the case in Canada (where Quebecers have been Prime Minister of the country for forty-two of the past fifty-three years – thus Quebecers who represent 22% of the population of Canada have held the top government position for 79% of the last five decades). The lesson from the former Soviet Union, the former Yugoslavia, Czechoslovakia, and most recently from East Timor is that artificial, imposed, and unwanted federations are not likely to last in the long-term. So, while the EU might indeed have been able to force the Cypriots to a deal, one must ask whether this would have been in anyone's long-term self-interest.

Partition may not be the only way to bring peace to Cyprus, but the international community, by taking partition off the table, may be proving itself stubborn and short-sighted.

Understanding these four myths and achieving balance in Cypriot communities are necessary foundations for any deal. Unfortunately, the perpetuation of the myths is exacerbating the situation on the island and making its puzzle much more difficult to solve.

PART III

Cyprus since 2004

"Something from Cyprus I may divine . . . it is a business of some heat"

SHAKESPEARE'S OTHELLO

CHAPTER 9

Turkey under the New Sultan

WHEN IT COMES TO REACHING a solution in Cyprus, the two primary veto holders are the Greek-Cypriot government and Turkey. Greece used to be part of the power dynamic, but the country's influence has dramatically waned. As a Canadian diplomat told us, the Greeks shafted Cyprus in the 2007-08 financial crisis, which was a blow to the *enosis* dream held by many Greek-Cypriots: "There is no party in Cyprus that now wants to join Greece."

Turkey's power and influence, on the other hand, have grown. President Erdoğan once seemed interested in helping to find a solution for Cyprus. There seemed to have been a window in 2004 when he would have considered a settlement, but that window closed. The Turkish government is now responsible for blocking prospects for a united Cyprus.

What changed? Turkey itself changed dramatically under Erdoğan's leadership, becoming an autocratic state. Sweden's V-Dem (Varieties of Democracy) Institute rates Turkey as an "electoral autocracy" whereas ten years ago they classified Turkey as an "electoral democracy". In 2020 Turkey ranked third on a V-Dem list of ten countries that have lost the most ground over the past ten years. On this list Turkey regressed less than Hungary and Poland but more than Brazil and India. Today Erdogan and the Turkish people are far less inclined to join the EU than they were eighteen years ago. As a result of these changes, Turkey pivoted away from the West, the EU, NATO, and the United States–organizations that had been applying pressure for a solution in Cyprus. Meanwhile, the EU itself changed substantially. Many of its members, as well as non-members, no longer see it as the great club it once was.

The changes within Turkey have been seismic. "In the lead up to 2004," says Harvard's Robert Rotberg, "Erdoğan had not consolidated his power."[123] He had come to office as the populist leader of the AKP, with a background in Islamist politics. He needed to marginalize the Turkish army which, perceiving itself as guardian of the nation's secular ideals, was suspicious of him. The risk of a coup was real: Turkey had experienced four military coups between 1960 and 1997. To this end, Erdoğan curried Western approval early in his career as prime minister. He scrapped Turkey's death penalty, allowed minority Kurdish language broadcasts, and made

---

123 Robert Rotberg, "Cyprus after Annan: Next Steps towards a Solution," *World Foundation Reports*, 37.

himself appear flexible on Cyprus. He was also far friendly to the idea of Turkey joining the EU than many had expected but it was consistent with his efforts to appear as a pro-Western moderate. The Turkish army was won over. The EU, however, was not.

After first applying for associate membership in the European Economic Community (EEC) in 1959, Turkey signed a customs union agreement with the EU in 1995, and began formal accession talks in October 2005 in Luxembourg. Simply getting to the talking stage was an enormous accomplishment. Erdoğan had brilliantly and bravely opened a door for the EU to waltz through. "Whereas parties that formed governments before the AKP often struggled to achieve a consensus on the merits of EU membership," says Professor Tozan Bahcheli, "the AKP, with its solid parliamentary majority, was uniquely in a position to achieve reforms and remove the remaining obstacles on the path to accession." The AKP's embrace of EU membership was "a political masterstroke that at one opportunity confounded their critics, averted a clash with the Turkish secular establishment, and even effectively shielded the AKP against a possible future military intervention"[124]

The Luxembourg talks were as far as Erdoğan would get. The EU sidelined Turkey and admitted members who applied years after it. It was clear that nothing was going to change to improve Turkey's chances in the near future. Erdoğan's strategy was blown up. He had assumed that if Turkish-Cypriots voted for a peaceful solution

124 Tozen Bahcheli and Sid Noel, "The rise of the AK Party and Ankara's Changing Role: Paving the way for the 'Yes'," in *Reunifying Cyprus*, eds. Varnava and Faustmann,235.

and Greek-Cypriots voted against, the isolation of Northern Cyprus would end, says former Turkish-Cypriot cabinet minister and peace negotiator Ozdil Nami. "He thought this would lead to rewards such as direct flights and that the Greek-Cypriots would not be able to block Turkey from getting into the EU. This betrayal led to disillusionment and a drifting away from the West."

The EU's rejection was indeed widely felt in Turkey. "Turks are very disappointed in EU politicians," says Nami. "They now see the EU as a Christian Club that will not let them in and so they have to explore alternatives."

The major alternative explored by Erdoğan after the EU failure was a sharp turn away from the West and towards illiberalism. Able to consolidate his power without EU membership, he took control of Turkey's most important institutions, "the military, the intelligence services, the police, the judiciary, the banks, the media, the election board, the mosques, and the educational system," says Daniel Pipes, president of the Middle East Forum. Erdoğan proved himself "a brilliant politician" and "Turkey's most consequential leader since Ataturk."[125]

Erdoğan now has his own private army and, like the sultans of the Ottoman Era, a 1,150-room palace. He is an autocrat, the supreme and sole decision maker in Turkey. He has purged opponents from the military, appointed partisan hacks to courts, and fired tens of thousands of teachers and civil servants. Ataturk's legacy of socialism and secularism has been repudiated. Today

125 Daniel Pipes, "Turkey may go the way of Venezuela," October 24, 2019, A15.

Turkey runs one of the world's largest prisons for journalists, second only to China in total numbers of jailed reporters.[126] Turkey ranks 153rd out of the 180 countries evaluated in the World Press Freedom Index (behind even Russia that ranks 150th). Wikipedia has been blocked in the country since 2017. Gay and transgender pride parades are banned. The country uses its own security forces and Syrian surrogates to target Kurds.

Religious education provides perhaps the best measure of Turkey's shift away from its secular history. One of the keys to its nineteenth-century Kemalist social reforms was a separation between church and state. In 2012, Turkey's religious schools, or Imam Hatip schools, had some 60,000 students in fewer than 500 facilities nationwide. Today that number has grown to 1.5 million students in over 4,000 schools.[127] Erdoğan himself is a graduate of an Imam Hatip school and in his drive to create a "pious Muslim" country, these schools receive double what the mainstream schools get in spending per pupil.

Turkey is a more muscular, confident and proud nation than it was in 2004, and a much more difficult challenge for the West. Whereas 71 percent of Turks supported joining the EU in 2004, that number had fallen to 49 percent by 2018 (it is even lower among AKP supporters). Only 20 percent of Turks believe that European governments want them in the EU.[128] This rejection has

126 *New York Times*, December 11, 2019
127 Soner Cagaptay, *The New Sultan* (London: I.B. Tauris, 2017), 190.
128 Max Hoffman, "A Snapshot of Turkish Public Opinion," *Center for American Progress*, September 27, 2018.

led to Turks themselves turning away from the EU. Diplomats in
Ankara and Brussels put on a brave face and continue the fantasy
that the EU might accept Turkey, but there is no clear path to
membership. As the *Economist* recently pointed out, "Turkey is
bigger than any EU country and its people are mostly Muslim.
Many European voters regard the prospect of such a nation joining the club with horror. So the chances are that the EU will not
accept Turkey whatever its democratic credentials. Signs of this
were present from the start of the membership talks in 2005."[129]
Says Soner Cagaptay in *The New Sultan*: "Today even liberal Turks
do not believe that the EU will ever deal them a fair hand, and
therefore almost no one in the country takes Europe seriously. The
joke in Turkey is that the country will become a EU member during Kosovo's presidential term in the EU—a dim prospect given
that Kosovo has yet to be recognized by all EU member states."[130]

Some would argue that the EU never wanted Turkey as a member, and there is evidence for this position. Manfred Weber, the
centrist leader of the European Peoples Party, said recently: "If I
become commission president then I will instruct the office in
Brussels to end the talks with Turkey on accession to the European
Union. Turkey cannot be a member of the European Union, let's
make that clear."[131] The *Economist* points out that "a German foreign minister remarked a few years ago, the EU will keep Turkey
out of the club as long as Mr Erdogan is in power. The truth is that

129 "Nowhere fast," *Economist*, August 28, 2021, 46.
130 Cagaptay, *The New Sultan*, 198.
131 Manfred Weber, *The Greek Observer*, March 6, 2019.

it will probably do so no matter who is in charge."[132] As one diplomat told us in Brussels, "we (the EU) pretend to negotiate and they (Turkey) pretend to reform." In March 2019, the European Parliament voted 370 to 109 to freeze Turkey's EU membership process. The move did not draw much attention because Turkey's membership process has been going nowhere for years, but many Turks saw it as a further demonstration of anti-Muslim attitudes in the EU.

Another unfortunate outcome of the EU's rejection of Turkey has been the destabilization of NATO. Turkey has been a key member of the alliance since 1954, a valuable bridge between East and West in the modern world. It is the only NATO country bordering two volatile countries, Syria and Iraq, and it has NATO's second largest army. Turkey is also home to critical American air assets, including some sixty to seventy nuclear bombs stored at Incirlik Air Base, and it is a key European partner in stemming the flow of refugees to the continent.

During a failed coup against his government, Erdoğan claimed that the United States was supporting his opponents and harboring their ringleader. He retaliated against the US by cutting power to the Incirlik Air Base, showing himself willing to endanger both his connection to the US and his standing in NATO.

Erdoğan further damaged his relationship with the U.S. and NATO by placing a $2.5 billion order for Russian S-400 missiles, notwithstanding an American offer to sell him patriot missiles.

---

132 "Nowhere fast," *Economist*, 46.

The S-400 missiles are a major concern for the US. Turkey was the world's third-largest customer for America's next generation F-35 fighter jets, making an order for 116 planes. The US cannot allow Turkey to have F-35s and S-400 missiles at the same time; possessing both pieces of sophisticated military technology would allow Turkey to configure the S-400 to track and defeat the F-35. In fact, Turkey is already using information from the S-400 missiles to track US-built fighters in its fleet, a significant problem for America and NATO.

Turkey meanwhile became more inclined to work with Russia than the West. From a historical perspective, this is an odd turn. As Soner Cagaptay points out: "For Turkish security analysts, no country is dreaded more for its military power and expansionist tendencies than Russia. Between 1568, when the Ottomans and Russians first clashed, and the end of the Russia Empire in 1917, the Turks and Russian fought over a dozen large scale wars."[133] Despite this historical animosity, recent polls show that 57 percent of Turks support building an alliance with Russia while only 55 percent want Turkey to remain in NATO. A recent PEW Research Study indicates that Turks feel more antipathy towards NATO than the U.S., Canada, and a dozen European nations. The antipathy predates the Trump administration. Only 25 percent had a favorable opinion of NATO in 2013; six years later, that number was 21 percent.

The Turkish perspective on the United States is still less favorable. Asked whether they trust the United States more than Russia,

133 Cagaptay, *The New Sultan*, 169.

or Russia more than the United States, 40 percent of Turks say they trust Russia more, and only 3 percent trust the US more. A January 2020 PEW poll found that only one in five Turks has a favorable opinion of the United States. The *Wall Street Journal* reported that "polls reliably indicate that 70 to 80 percent of Turks regard the US as a hostile power. While anti-Americanism is an old story in Turkey, in recent years it has taken on a sharper edge. Turks increasingly see America as a threat."[134]

The change is due to a number of factors. In 2019, the United States Senate and the House of Representatives both recognized the Armenian genocide of 1915. Congress also voted to restrict arms sales to Turkey. In October 2019, New York prosecutors indicted state-owned Halkbank, one of Turkey's biggest state lenders, for bypassing American sanctions against Iran. This apparent gold-for-oil scheme transferred some $20-billion in restricted Iranian funds to intermediaries connected to senior Ministers in Erdoğan's AKP Party.

The implications of these fractured relationships are alarming for the U.S., NATO, and the West. They are also troublesome for Cyprus. As Turkey moves away from the West, it will have less reason to compromise on the island's future. Indeed, it has not refrained from complicating matters. Erdoğan has injected a religious element into a conflict that historically has been primarily ethnic. Turkish-Cypriots are not happy about this. Among the least religious people in the Muslim world, they resist Turkey's

---

134 Michael Doran and Mike Reynolds, "Turkey has Legitimate Grievances against the US," *Wall Street Journal*, October 9, 2019, A17.

attempted "Islamification" of Northern Cyprus. They have staged large protests against Turkey's backslide into authoritarianism and chafed against Erdoğan's latest incursion into their island—a $13-million mosque between Nicosia and Famagusta. The vast majority of Turkish-Cypriots see themselves as Cypriot first, and 75 percent of them wholly reject annexation by Turkey. But Erdoğan's incursions have nevertheless had an impact. By accentuating differences between north and south in Cyprus, Erdoğan has wedged the two sides apart and empowered Greek-Cyprus to reject compromise.

With EU membership off the table, no Western power is positioned to coax Turkey toward compromise. Brussels has no leverage, and no individual EU members are close to Ankara. The US is out of the picture, as is Great Britain, having left the EU. The Turks are likely to be satisfied with the status quo in Cyprus indefinitely.

Erdoğan appears to be enjoying his newfound independence. Much like Russia, Turkey still thinks of itself as a great power, deserving a place at the head table with the world's leaders. "The collapse of the Ottoman Empire continues to shape Turkey's view of its place in the world," says Soner Cagaptay, "creating myths and goals that resonate in the Turkish psyche. Nations that were great empires never forget that fact, and they often have a malleable, exaggerated sense of their glory days and a story about why they are no longer an empire."[135]

---

135 Cagaptay, *The New Sultan*, 7.

In 2020, Erdoğan made some headway in asserting Turkey as a serious power-broker, giving us a glimpse of what could be a new world order in the Middle East: when a ceasefire was finally agreed upon in the longstanding Libyan conflict, it was Turkey and Russia that negotiated the deal rather than the U.S. and the Europeans. Turkey has since found other opportunities to throw its weight around the Middle East and influence the region's politics. It is becoming a significant player on the Eastern Mediterranean energy scene.

There are limits to Erdoğan's independence. Turkey must stay on speaking terms with the EU, an important trading partner. The Turkish economy went through difficult times in 2018 due to rapidly escalating food prices, inflation close to 25 percent, and unemployment that skyrocketed from 3.2 million in July 2018 to 4.5 million in July 2019. In June 2021 inflation remained at 17.5%.[136] These issues have been exasperated by a serious depreciation of the Turkish Lira as the Lira has lost close to 80% of its value relative to the US dollar since 2001.[137] Fortunately for Erdoğan, his need for economic access to Europe is balanced by the EU's need for Turkey's help with its refugee crisis. Turkey, which is eight times the size of Greece hosts more than 80 times the number of refugees including some 3.7 million Syrians.[138] In these basic ways, the EU needs Turkey, and Turkey needs the EU, but neither side wants to take the relationship any further.

136 "Pick a number," *Economist*, July 31, 2021, 59.
137 "Scandals galore," *Economist*, July 10, 2021, 49.
138 "At 70, the global convention on refugees is needed more than ever," *Economist*, August 7, 2021, 50.

The bottom line is that the EU missed a golden opportunity to make a Cyprus deal in 2004, and it may not get another one. "Neither the EU nor the US understood Erdoğan's political courage in 2004 when he pushed for a Cyprus settlement," says Ozdil Nami. The door is now closed. Turkey is a very different country, and the stakes are higher and more sensitive.

CHAPTER 10

Russia's Role in Cyprus

RUSSIA'S SOFT POWER CAMPAIGN in the Republic of Cyprus stretches back to the Cold War and has stymied progress on a solution for Greek-Cypriots and Turkish-Cypriots by exploiting the island's divisions and tensions. Occasionally, as when Russian ambassador Stanislav Osadichy attended a seminar in Nicosia attacking the peace process, Russia's attempts at destabilization are blatant. However, Russia's often invisible influence on the island better serves its ultimate purpose: causing rifts within Western coalitions such as NATO and the EU. It is worth understanding the history of Russian influence in Cyprus and the impact of this relationship on the EU, because these are significant obstacles to resolving the island's problems.

Russia and Cyprus emphasize their shared connection to the Orthodox faith as the foundation of their relationship. In both countries, the Orthodox Church maintains a strong grip on social and political life. Greek-Cypriots have looked to the Orthodox

Church as a leader in government, war, and times of crisis, such as when Archbishop Makarios led the opposition to British colonial rule of the island. Makarios served as both archbishop and president of the Republic of Cyprus from 1960 to his death in 1977, illustrating that the Orthodox faith is inextricably linked to Cypriot political power.

Putin and his government make it a point to stress their own connection to the Orthodox Church, and Putin frequently visits sites sacred to the Orthodox faith when traveling abroad. This is largely about optics. When Russia meddles in the affairs of nations with an Orthodox religious foundation, it masks its geopolitical ambitions with the benign language of culture. Following a meeting in Moscow with his Greek-Cypriot counterpart Nicos Christodoulides, Russian foreign minister Sergey Lavrov asserted that his nation's support for Cyprus is "based on traditional links of friendship and mutual sympathy, spiritual and cultural affinity." At the same time, Russia and the Orthodox Church have supported the far-right ELAM party in recent elections, which has *enosis* with Greece as its stated platform. Russia uses its Orthodox background to show a friendly face to the Cypriots while also giving legitimacy to its most extreme factions and bolstering opposition to a negotiated settlement.

Russia, a large power with a permanent seat on the UN Security Council, is an enormous asset for the Greek-Cypriots: it exclusively supports them in negotiations with Turkish-Cypriots and guarantor powers, and reinforces the status quo of an effective Greek-Cypriot ethno-state. Without Russia, the demands of the Greek-Cypriots would carry far less weight. At the same time,

Cyprus gives Russia a foothold in the EU. Russia and Cyprus have recently collaborated to meet mutually beneficial ends. "In 2004, Moscow vetoed a proposed Security Council resolution that would have provided certain security guarantees designed to underpin the Annan Plan," writes Dr. James Ker-Lindsay in *The Cyprus Problem: What Everyone Needs to Know*. "Although the Greek-Cypriots denied that this move was made at their behest, the weight of the evidence suggests otherwise. Cypriot President Tassos Papadopoulos and Russia had coordinated to discredit the Annan Plan; by foiling reunification, Russia hurt Turkey's route to EU accession. Russia then . . . embarked on a campaign of bringing Turkey closer to Russia, all as a means of weakening international governing bodies meant to constrain Russian power."[139]

Russia has not sought a resolution of the island's division because it loves nothing more than destabilizing NATO and its members. "[Russians] are just trouble makers in Cyprus," says Lord David Hannay, the UN special representative to Cyprus from 1996-2003. "They just stir the pot. NATO is their enemy so they support Greek-Cypriots because that causes headaches for the West and NATO."

The fact that Russia and Cyprus scratch each other's backs has led to Cyprus maintaining a permissive stance on the Russian Federation's aggression towards its neighbors. This permissiveness extends to Cyprus' decision-making at the UN. In 2009, Cyprus was the only EU member-state that did not vote in favor of

---

139 James Ker-Lindsay, *The Cyprus Problem: What everyone needs to know* (Oxford: Oxford University Press, 2011), 98.

Georgian refugees' right of return after Russia's onslaught against Georgia in the August 2008 war. The conflict displaced 192,000 Georgians, but Cyprus, then led by the left-wing AKEL party, chose to abstain. The opposition DISY party blasted the decision, citing "not wanting to annoy Russia" as the main reason behind AKEL's stance. Greek-Cypriots do not see the hypocrisy of supporting Russia's right to hostile land annexation, says Dr. Ker-Lindsay. They decry Turkey's presence on their island since 1974 as an invasion, but then turn around and defend the largest land grab since World War II by their strongest and most vocal supporter.

The collapse of the Soviet Union in 1991 added a new dimension to Cypriot-Russian relations. The rapid privatization of Russian businesses after the fall of Communism birthed the so-called oligarch class in Russia. Former government officials were able to acquire assets previously owned by the state, bilking the Russian people out of billions of rubles. Rather than investing in Russia, these newly wealthy individuals stored their financial assets in off-shore bank accounts, out of the reach of the government. Putin and the Kremlin are aware of this arrangement, and enable it so long as the oligarchs remain loyal.

As the Panama Papers revealed, Cyprus is a hub of offshore Russian banking. The island's reputation as a preeminent home of offshore accounts was enhanced when Lebanon fought a severe civil war. Cyprus positioned itself as a safe alternative to Beirut. Putin's inner circle now uses Cyprus to hide its money, and many believe that Putin himself is a participant in this scheme. (Followers of American politics will undoubtedly be familiar with the names

Paul Manafort, Oleg Deripaska, and Viktor Vekselberg, all of whom were revealed to have offshore accounts in Cyprus.)

Not only Russian money made its way to Cyprus. Russians began emigrating to the island in the 1990s, following the fall of the Soviet Union. The southern Cypriot city of Limassol is home to so many Russian nationals and Russian-speaking Cypriots that they call it "Limassolgrad."

It follows that Cyprus is a willing beneficiary of this money-laundering. Cypriot lawyers and accountants visit trade shows to tout their country's low tax rate and lax approach to supervision. Russian and Ukrainian business registrations have flourished in Cyprus, and Cypriot banks have done all they can to make their clients feel welcome. Legal and accounting firms have become expert in moving Russian financial assets from Russia to Cyprus, and introducing Russian clients to Cypriot politicians. The island's biggest law firms, says Dr. Panicos Demetriades, former governor of the Bank of Cyprus, "are politically connected, including the president's family law firm. The top five law firms, they've made millions and millions from Russians basically, to put it politely, to optimize their tax affairs."

Cyprus made cosmetic changes to this business relationship when it sought EU membership in the early 2000s. Cyprus' EU accession process was contingent on it tightening up its rules on money laundering. The banks and law firms shifted their emphasis to boasting of Cyprus's 10 percent corporate tax rate, the lowest in Europe, and continued its practices. The Cypriot financial industry is now deeply invested in maintaining a clean appearance without interrupting the flow of money. Cypriot lawyers represent their Russian clients in court and employ their connections to help politicians turn a blind eye to their activities.

At the beginning of the Euro Crisis in late 2012, *Der Spiegel* published a scathing article on the EU's bailout of failing Cypriot banks and, by extension, their Russian clients. Journalists Markus Dettmer and Christian Reierman revealed that "a secret report written by the German foreign intelligence service . . . outlines who would be the main beneficiaries of the billions of euros of European taxpayers' money: Russian oligarchs, businessmen, and Mafiosi who have invested their illegal money in Cyprus."[140]

The EU is wary of the bond between Cyprus and Russia, which endangers its unity. In January 2020, the EU agreed to blacklist officials in Crimea tied to its annexation by Russia in 2014, but this move was blocked by the Cypriots. Because EU sanctions require unanimous support from all twenty-eight nations, Cyprus has used its veto both on the Crimea and to back Russia's unilateral seizure of Ukrainian territory. An EU diplomat expressed frustration about this dynamic, claiming that Cyprus' defiant position is "all the more surprising since Cyprus has enjoyed unparalleled solidarity from its EU partners" over its dispute with Turkey.

The corrupt links between Cyprus and Russia extend to the senior-most politicians. Two out of Cyprus' three most recent presidents have been involved in the Cypriot legal industry and its questionable foreign connections. The first of these three, Tassos Papadopolous (2003-2008), was a lawyer and chair of the

---

140 Markus Dettmer and Christian Reiermann, "bailing out Oligarchs: EU Aid to Cyprus a Political Minefield for Merkel," *Der Spiegel*, November 5, 2012.

Cypriot parliament's foreign affairs committee in 1995 when his firm was cited by the United States Treasury as "a front for Serbian businesses."[141]

Papadopolous's successor, the late Demetris Christofias (2008-2013), was the EU's first and only openly communist leader. Christofias earned a degree in history at Moscow's Institute of Social Sciences and adopted a pro-Soviet outlook. His political career collapsed during the Euro Crisis of 2013.

Christofias' successor, President Nicos Anastasiades (2013-present), was another successful lawyer before transitioning into politics. His former firm in Limassol, Nicos Chr. Anastasiades and Partners LLC, still bears his name and employs his daughters. It specializes in banking for Russian businessmen and helping them to acquire "golden passports." The golden passport concept works like this: if a non-EU resident makes a sufficient investment in Cypriot real estate, he or she is able to obtain an EU passport. Cyprus manages this by skirting an EU rule that requires "effective" residency in an EU state before applying for citizenship. (The country is estimated to have raked in €5 billion, mostly in the form of real estate investment, by granting coveted EU passports for around €2 million apiece.) A 2019 report from the European Commission cites this scheme, conducted in Cyprus as well as Malta and Bulgaria, as invitations for money laundering and organized crime.[142]

---

141 Chris Hedges, "Cyprus shores wash dirty money," *New York Times*, June 15, 1995.

142 Francesco Guarascio, "EU warns of crime risks from governments' sales of passports, visas," *Reuters*, January 23, 2019.

The EU has begun to crack down on the practice. Since the EC's 2019 report, Bulgaria no longer offers a golden passport. Anastasiades has come under fire from his own government for his role in these schemes; in early 2019, the Republic of Cyprus' house watchdog committee opened an investigation into Anastasiades' family ties to golden passports. The house investigation was triggered when the newspaper *Haravghi* reported that Victor Pichugov, formerly Russia's ninth richest man, had been granted a Cypriot passport by investing in Cypriot real estate. Pichugov was once a major shareholder in the state-backed Russian bank Promsvyazbank, which erected Promsvyazbank Tower in Limassol in June 2012. Imperio Properties, the Cypriot investment firm that oversaw the project, is co-owned by Anastasiades' son-in-law. In December 2018, Pichugov and his wife became Cypriot citizens.[143]

President Anastasiades has been rather defensive about this issue, declaring that he will resign should any links between him and the program be found (being father to his daughters does not constitute a link in his mind). He has attacked the EU and defended what he considers a legitimate investment program. Speaking to *Haravghi*, the outlet that linked him to the scheme, Anastasiades said: "It is a programme which led to the construction sector to recovery, employed a large number of workers, and contributed

---

143 Imperio Properties maintains that the deal was legitimate because Pichugov did not buy shares in Promsvyazbank until after the tower was built. Anastasiades' law firm and Imperio Properties both tout the "Cyprus Investment Programme" as a reason to do business with them. To use their words, "this is a unique opportunity to convert business activities to European citizenship with all the benefits."

to the revival of the economy and growth."[144] This growth has largely been confined to Limassol. The villas around the city's ritzy marina sit empty while locals can no longer afford skyrocketing rents. In June 2018, a group called "Limassol for All" organized a protest over the 25 percent spike in housing costs in just two years; approximately one thousand people joined the march.

Anastasiades' defensive reaction to global scrutiny of the golden passport scandal suggests that he does, in fact, have a personal stake in both the "investment programme" and in maintaining a good relationship with Vladimir Putin, even at the cost of injuring his relationship with the EU, and the interests of the majority of Cypriots.

President Anastasiades' desire to maintain the economic engine by which Cypriot law firms (including his own) promote Russian investment in the island makes him fundamentally incapable of taking the necessary steps to make Cyprus compliant with EU money laundering laws. He has so far maintained his family business in the face of international sanctions on Russia, and appeased President Putin at the same time.

The fact remains that Russia now has a rare friend on Europe's eastern periphery, and it will not easily give it up. It has embedded itself in Cypriot culture and the island's government. Well-positioned to influence Cypriot politics, it will oppose any efforts to find a potential solution between Greek-Cypriots and Turkish-Cypriots. This position goes back to those cultural ties

144 Reprinted from Haravghi, "President defends golden visa scheme," *Cyprus Mail,* March 11, 2019.

we introduced at the beginning of the chapter. The Russians are building Orthodox churches on the island and turning Cyprus into their "holiday satellite country," says Dr. Demetriades. They feel an affinity with the island, at least its southern reaches. Two Russian oligarchs even tried to get a political party off the ground in Cyprus. It was called the "I, the Citizen" party, and it vowed to represent Russian-speaking Cypriots and run in the 2019 European Parliamentary elections. Although these ambitions fizzled, Russia has more than enough financial ties to Cyprus to have significant and lasting political clout.

Another reason that Russia doesn't want a solution between the two Cypriot communities is that it would have to contend with the influence of both Islam and Turkey, a NATO power. A solution also would allow the EU and NATO to sort themselves out and pat themselves on the back, and give Turkey an easier path to the development of a gas pipeline. Far better, from Putin's point of view, to keep the island divided. He exacerbates tensions by giving Greek-Cypriots full support for whatever they desire, be it a no vote on the Annan Plan, or a vote for an extension of the UN's peacekeeping mission on the island.

Cyprus is a pawn on a much larger chessboard where Putin can encourage NATO powers like Greece, Great Britain, and Turkey to fight one another and destabilize a peaceful world order. It is a strategy from the same playbook that Putin has used in other parts of the world, most visibly in 2016's American presidential elections.

CHAPTER 11

Natural Gas:
The Mixed Blessing

THE PAST DECADE HAS SEEN a flurry of interest in the energy reserves of the eastern Mediterranean Sea. The Republic of Cyprus's political hopes for this gas have been high since 2008, when it signed an exploratory agreement with the American energy giant Noble Energy to search for energy reserves in the Aphrodite Field, which sits at the southern edge of Cyprus' exclusive economic zone (EEZ). In the years since, these hopes have dimmed with the realization that the discovery of gas has exacerbated rather than soothed the differences between Greek and Turkish-Cypriots. This was perhaps a predictable outcome. We have seen in Nigeria, Venezuela, and Saudi Arabia that a country's dependency on energy reserves is no guarantee of peace and stability.

Another reason hopes have dimmed is that the volumes of gas in the Aphrodite Field now appear smaller than originally estimated. It is estimated to contain about 129 billion cubic metres (bcm) of natural gas. ExxonMobil announced in February 2019 that it had found between 141.6 bcm and 226.5 bcm in another part of the EEZ. The CEO of Italian energy company Eni, Claudio Descalzi, has said that a third site in the EEZ contains between 170 and 230 bcm of gas. These amounts are potentially useful, but they do not justify major investment. Charles Ellinas of the Atlantic Council's Global Energy Center says ExxonMobil will consider building an LNG plant in Cyprus if it finds between 283.2 bcm and 424.75 bcm of gas.

Egypt's Zohr gas field, which has been the Eastern Mediterranean's biggest success story to date and is already feeding Egypt's growing needs, contains around 850 bcm. Output from Zohr began in December 2017 and as of late 2018, Egypt now boasts two LNG plants at Idku and Damietta; it has the necessary infrastructure and is now exporting significant volumes of gas. Cyprus, as of yet, does not appear to have been comparably blessed by natural geography.

Former TRNC Minister of Finance Serdar Denktaş says that "the gas numbers for Cyprus are exaggerated. There is only enough for Cyprus itself and not for export." Jack Straw, the former British foreign minister, agrees: "Given the amount of gas, it makes limited sense to build [an] LNG [plant] in Cyprus and at this stage it is not clear how commercial its gas would be."

As of yet, Greek-Cypriots have not heeded calls to temper their expectations for a Cypriot gas industry. They have granted drilling licenses and created multinational agreements with Egypt, Lebanon, Israel, Italy, France, and the United States. Speaking to reporters in New York in May 2019, Cypriot Energy Minister Giorgios Lakkotrypis said that Cyprus expected to begin exporting natural gas from the Aphrodite Field in 2025. A month later, Lakkotrypis backtracked with another statement that lowered the revenues expected from gas deals by more than half to $520 million per year, but this decline was attributed to low global gas prices, not the scale or feasibility of the project.

Turkish-Cypriots have been excluded from the licensing meetings between the Greek-Cypriot government and international energy companies. Ödzil Nami, former foreign minister and minister for the economy and energy of the TRNC, said of his Greek-Cypriot counterparts, "now they have a new toy and they want to play with it: hydrocarbons." Turkey has responded by harassing foreign drilling vessels, despite soft EU sanctions and American warnings to cease and desist. That tensions in Cyprus have escalated over a relatively small slice of the global natural gas market is unfortunate and unnecessary. Fortunately, there are signs that both sides are coming to their senses.

Turkish-Cypriot President Mustafa Akıncı extended an olive branch when he told the press, "In this region, economic cooperation is needed as in other areas. If a satisfactory quantity of gas is found, the most reasonable route is to reach Europe via Turkey. Greek-Cypriots themselves agree with this. The international community should pat the back of the Greek-Cypriot side. . . . Wealth must be exploited jointly. In case of co-operation, the Greek-Cypriot community will live friendly with a large 80 million country otherwise new tensions will be created."[145]

145 "Anatasiades says no Cyprus Unity talks while Turkey drills," *TheNationalHerald.com*, July 30, 2019.

His Greek-Cypriot counterpart President Nicos Anastasiades has also shown more flexibility, in all likelihood an acknowledgment that he no longer believes Cyprus' gas reserves are especially lucrative. Anastasiades has suggested a profit-sharing agreement with Turkish-Cypriots that would take place if Turkey agreed to stop its gunboat diplomacy. This is a significant step forward, if Anastasiades holds to his proposal.

The discovery and development of Aphrodite gas is playing out amid a broader global battle to lessen dependence on fossil fuels. In 2009, the European Union asked its member states to set their own energy targets with the ultimate goal of deriving 20 percent of their final energy consumption from renewables by 2020. Due to its lack of energy infrastructure and isolated location, it is unsurprising that Cyprus has struggled to meet these goals, according to the latest report from the EU. In 2012, nearly 95 percent of Cyprus' fuel needs were imported in the form of petroleum products. Though LNG is not a renewable source of energy, it burns cleaner than oil and its importation will help Cyprus stave off carbon-emission penalties from the EU.

In 2019, energy minister Lakkotrypis signed a €290 million deal to build an LNG plant in Cyprus to import energy to the island: €110 million of the total cost will be funded by the EU, with Cyprus' Electricity Authority (EAC) and the European Bank for Reconstruction and Development covering the remainder. This will keep the lights on in Cyprus for the foreseeable future and help to meet the EU benchmarks. But the longer-term problem remains that it has placed all its bets on hydrocarbons to the complete exclusion of solar, wind, and other renewable sources.

That the LNG plant is being built is not a sign of sustainable future energy wealth for Cyprus. It is for buying, not for selling gas. In 2013, experts looked into building an LNG plant for export at Vasilikos on the south coast of the island, but the plan was scrapped due to its economic infeasibility. There is simply not enough gas off the Cypriot coast to be economically viable.

Should that somehow change and the Aphrodite field yield enough gas for Cyprus to export, its marketability, in any event, would be limited. The EU's emphasis on renewables is one problem. The dependence of EU members on Russian for what gas volumes they require is another. Germany, for instance, boasts renewables as the source of 44 percent of its electricity consumption. For the time being, fluctuations in wind farm outputs have caused power prices to skyrocket for German consumers. To keep their economy running and to prevent shortages, Germany imports 40 percent of its oil and 35 percent of its gas from Russia. In 2018, Germany's natural gas imports from Russia rose 12 percent over 2017 levels. Because Germany needs to import 92 percent of its natural gas, we can expect that this number will increase in coming years.

Berlin has deepened its energy ties with Russia through the soon-to-be-completed Nord Stream 2 pipeline between Russia and Germany. Nord Stream 2, a 1,200-km behemoth that will connect the world's largest gas reserves to Europe, will power about 26 million households per year. It's a political headache for Germany to deal so closely with a geopolitical adversary, but it is a necessity at present.

Cyprus has a fraction of Russia's gas bounty and none of its infrastructure, so it is highly implausible for European nations to look at Eastern Mediterranean gas as an alternative to Russia. The IEA's latest report states that the United States, Australia, and Russia will lead the world in global gas exports by 2024, with the US expected to export more than Australia and Russia combined.[146]

That stiff competition is another argument for Cyprus to lower its expectations for its off-shore wells to bring wealth beyond its own energy needs.

Cypriot gas ultimately suffers from four major problems: there is not enough of it, it is expensive to get at; it will be costly to get to market; and it lies in the middle of disputed territory. Even if Cyprus did have enough gas to make it an attractive site for energy export, its most likely market would be Turkey, which needs to reduce its imports and its huge annual energy bill. Given the proximity of the two nations, it seems to be a logical recipient for any Cypriot gas surplus. But given Turkey's increasingly militaristic impulses, the region's historic instability, and continued tensions on the island, investors are unlikely to get involved in this quagmire.

"Because of Turkey's actions in the EEZ," says Fiona Mullen, director of the Nicosia-based Sapienta Economics, "it is not certain that Cyprus will be able to sell gas . . . Only a political solution will end this."[147]

"At the end," concurs Jack Straw, "Turkey will not allow the gas to be exploited unless there is an agreed deal."

---

146 "Top 5 Natural Gas Producers in the World," *EnergyCentral.com*, May 20, 2019.
147 Chloe Emmanouilides, "Gas in Cyprus:blessing or curse?," *Osservatorio BalcaniCaucaso. org*, January 1, 2019.

Dr. Charles Ellinas, senior fellow of the Global Energy Center at the Atlantic Council, and Dr. Hubert Faustmann, professor of history and international relations at the University of Nicosia, maintain that the best-case scenario for the Aphrodite Field is that an American company finds enough gas to invest in building a pipeline or an LNG (liquified natural gas) plant. The company could use its leverage to press for a solution that benefits both of Cyprus' communities and Turkey, which is still a NATO ally. This will create calmer conditions in the region and allow international companies to invest and explore for hydrocarbons in peace. It might be enough to break the current stalemate on the island: new peace talks could center on the possibility of a pipeline through Turkey and shared input into a licensing agreement.

One would think that the possibility of energy wealth would be an excellent reason for Greek and Turkish-Cypriots to resolve their differences and not become yet another hotspot in the Eastern Mediterranean, but as Hubert Faustmann correctly points out: "In the Eastern Mediterranean, politics trumps economics".

CHAPTER 12

Demographics of Cyprus

ISTORICALLY, CYPRUS HAS BEEN home to two dominant groups, Greek-Cypriots and Turkish-Cypriots, and smaller numbers of Armenians and Maronites (a Christian sect of Syrian origin in communion with the Roman Catholic Church). Whether in the context of British imperial mandates that empowered Turkish-Cypriots to have a greater say in local politics or ethnic cleansing campaigns conducted by Greek-Cypriots and leading to the 1974 division of the island, there are few debates in Cyprus in which demographics do not play a role.

After nearly half a century living apart, the schism between Greek and Turkish-Cypriots is deep and likely insurmountable. Following independence in 1960, amidst a global backdrop of drawing national lines based on ethnic self-determination, the Republic of Cyprus, population 573,000, was an uneasy union of two groups different in every respect: ethnic origin, language, and religion (Greek Orthodox and Sunni Muslim). Those differences are evident in pre-1974 demographic maps showing Greek and Turkish-Cypriots living not in intercommunal fashion, as some mythologizers have it, but in homogeneous enclaves.[148]

In the present day, the demographics of both the Republic of Cyprus and the Turkish Republic of Northern Cyprus (TRNC) have shifted significantly, and not in a way that is conducive to reunification. As of the last census in 2011, the Republic of Cyprus (the Greek Cypriot-governed portion of the island) had a population of approximately 840,407. More recent estimates put the total population of the Republic of Cyprus at 1.2 million.[149] A full 99% of the population is Greek-Cypriot. There are non-citizens from other EU countries, particularly Greece and Great Britain.

Over time, the Republic of Cyprus has become increasingly international, cosmopolitan, and prosperous. Much of the republic's dynamism is attributable to youth: 62 percent of the population is below the age of 45. In fact, the median age of Greek-Cypriots is only 35.4 years-old.

Because the number of Greek-Cypriots who experienced pre-1974 life on the island is decreasing, the republic's citizens are less accustomed to dealing directly with Turkish-Cypriots. The young think of the Turkish-Cypriots as aliens and prefer the status quo. A study conducted after the collapse of the Annan Plan in 2004 showed that 41 percent of Greek-Cypriots aged 18 to 24

---

148 Ricahard A. Patrick, *Political Geography and the Cyprus Conflict, 1963-1971* (Waterloo, Ontario: Department of Geography Publications, University of waterloo, 1978), 78.

149 "UN Demographic Yearbook: Table 7," *UN Statistics Division*, accessed August 17, 2019.

want a permanent division of the island, as opposed to just 10 percent of Greek-Cypriots aged 55-65.[150] In a survey conducted by the authors in 2019 only 37 percent of Greek-Cypriots under age 35 said they would vote yes in a referendum to re-unite the island compared to 67 percent of those older than 55. The older Greek-Cypriots are significantly more interested in unification as they reminisce about the good old days when they were masters of the entire island. In another decade, as the generation gap grows, even fewer people living in the south will seek a reunified island— something they've never known.

Population data from the Turkish Republic of Northern Cyprus is scarce because Turkey's President Erdoğan has blocked a census in the region. It is believed there are 90,000 to 100,000 Turkish-Cypriots, and anywhere from 99,000 to 102,000 "settlers" and temporary residents from Turkey (this includes students but does not include the 35,000 members of the Turkish Army and their families).[151]

Older Turkish-Cypriots, those who remember the years before 1974, prefer a divided island. Unlike the younger Greek-Cypriots the younger Turkish-Cypriots are more supportive of a bi-zonal, bi-communal deal. Unfortunately for the prospects of such a deal, increasing numbers of young Turkish-Cypriots are emigrating to

150 Craig Webster, "Division or Unification in Cyprus? The role of demographics, attitudes and party inclination on Greek Cypriot preferences for a solution to the Cyprus problem," *Ethnopolitics*, Vol 4, No. 3, September 2005, 307.

151 Mete Hatay, "Beyond Numbers: An Inquiry into the Political Integration of the Turkish 'Settlers' in Northern Cyprus," *PRIO Report 4/2005* (Oslo: International Peace Research Institute, Oslo (PRIO)), viii.

Turkey and elsewhere in search of more fruitful opportunities. That makes the TRNC's population relatively older and less likely to strike a deal.

The issue of the settlers is bitterly contested in Cyprus. The term itself is contentious and often pejorative, because it refers to the Turkish nationals who now outnumber Turkish-Cypriots. Greek-Cypriots have accused Turkey of fomenting demographic change on the island, which they allege is a violation of the Geneva Convention which says occupying forces are not allowed to move their own civilians into occupied territories. Because Greek-Cypriots maintain that the Turkish invasion of 1974 and occupation of the northern 37 percent of the island are illegal acts, the allegation is not unreasonable.

In the recent comedy film *Smuggling Hendrix* (2018), which won the top prize in the international category at the Tribeca Film Festival, Greek-Cypriot director Marios Piperides told the story of a musician named Yiannis whose dog Jimi crosses the buffer zone into the Turkish-Cypriot side of Nicosia. As Yiannis tries to bring Jimi (now trapped in the north due to European laws) back home, he encounters the settlers who have moved into his family's old home and befriends their Cyprus-born son, Hasan. Throughout, Piperides emphasizes common humanity and the ridiculousness of bureaucracy, especially in a scene where Hasan cannot get a Cypriot passport because he's the son of an "occupier."

The *Cyprus Mail* review of the film predictably states, "a viewer who knows nothing of Cyprus might also come to some awkward conclusions. They might conclude, for instance, that the most victimized and hard-done-by group on the island are the Turkish settlers, resented by both sides through no fault of their own."[152] For Greek-Cypriots, humanizing Turkish settlers means acknowledging that they are not alone in suffering from the island's conflicts. Turkish-Cypriots view the settlers as outnumbering them in what was meant to be their safe haven. Since Turkish settlers are an issue in all peace negotiations, we must understand this group and how it affects the dynamics on the island.

Following independence, the respective populations of Greek and Turkish-Cypriots determined the balance of political power, and Greek-Cypriots were especially concerned that the quotas for state hiring exceeded the actual numbers of Turkish-Cypriots. In a bitter irony, Turkish-Cypriot population numbers did, in fact, grow, but largely as a consequence of Greek-Cypriot brutality. Under threat and displaced from their homes, the Turkish-Cypriots, turned to Turkey for assistance in 1974. The Turkish invasion led to the first wave of immigration from Turkey, which was initially welcomed by Turkish-Cypriots because they needed to sustain an economy entirely dependent on Turkey.

In addition to Turkish-Cypriot citizenship, the Turkish immigrants received the homes abandoned by Greek-Cypriots fleeing the Turkish invasion. For Greek-Cypriots, these property issues remain front-and-centre in peace negotiations; they insist upon the return of land and houses they once owned. In that demand,

---

152 Preston Wilder, "Film review: Smuggling Hendrix," *CyprusMail.com*, May 13, 2019.

Greek-Cypriots have the full backing of the international community, which is evident in the payouts that the European Court of Human Rights demands from Turkey.

Since 1974, the Republic of Cyprus has accused Turkey of wanting to increase the Turkish population in the north in order to affect elections. Fear of being swamped by newcomers has led the Greek-Cypriots to allow Turkish-Cypriots to register for Cypriot passports and vote in elections in the Republic of Cyprus while barring so-called settlers from doing the same. It is not fair to think of these people as foreign invaders, especially the settlers of today. Mete Hatay argues that while the first wave of immigrants from Turkey can realistically be called settlers, their children and grandchildren have never known Turkey and consider themselves Turkish-Cypriots.

It is difficult to ascertain how many settlers there are in the TRNC both because Erdoğan will not allow a census and because after nearly fifty years together, many Turkish-Cypriots have married Turkish nationals. Mixed families are common. Any future solution must include a reliable census of Northern Cyprus and a proposal for how to integrate Turkish nationals.

It is not only the Greek-Cypriots who are wary of settlers. Ozdil Nami explained to us that "every month a thousand new Turkish workers come to Cyprus . . . and they do not go back to Turkey. They demand TRNC citizenship and their children have never been to Turkey. This is speeding up the rate of change."

In 2002, *The Telegraph* published a report on Turkish-Cypriot sentiments regarding settlers and ended on an ominous note: "Three decades later Turkish-Cypriots are in danger of disappearing

altogether."[153] One of the sources for the article estimated that
1,000 Turkish-Cypriots were emigrating from the TRNC each
month as farmers from Anatolia moved in.

The remaining Turkish-Cypriot population is deeply uninterested in becoming a satellite Turkish state. One of the largest
fears that Turkish-Cypriots have about the ongoing transforma-
tion of their home is that Turkish nationals are considerably more
religious than they are. Most Turkish-Cypriots are nominally
Sunni Muslims, but many do not practice. It is uncommon to see
Turkish-Cypriot women wearing headscarves or Turkish-Cypriots
of any gender abstaining from alcohol. The Turkish-Cypriots, like
the Greek-Cypriots, are concerned about Erdoğan's latest initiative
to build immense mosques in the north. For Turkish-Cypriots,
there is fear that a more visible form of Islam will take root and
become a further impediment to reconciliation with the Greek
Orthodox south.

(Interestingly, the Turkish-Cypriots share a religious disconnect
with many Greek-Cypriots. Although 96 percent of Greek-Cypriots
identify with the Greek Orthodox Church, a 1998 opinion poll
indicated that less than half of them attend church regularly.[154]
However, the leaders of the Greek Orthodox Church play a significant role in Greek-Cypriot politics in a way that imams do not
in the TRNC. If half the Greek-Cypriot population is not deeply

153 Tabitha Morgan, "Turkish Cypriots leave island as 'settlers' move in," *The Telegraph*,
      September 7, 2002.
154 "Cyprus: International Relations Freedom Report 2002; Bureau of Democracy,
      Human Rights and Labor," *USStateDepartment.gov*, 2002.

invested in religious life, you wouldn't know it from the island's political results.)

When you're actually on the street in Cyprus, demographics become more complicated. In the south, the island's tensions are highlighted by certain monuments and pieces of public art.

Passing through the UN buffer zone from Turkish-Cypriot Lefkoşa to Greek-Cypriot Nicosia, one sees many graffiti tags in support of a united Cyprus, but these are overwhelmed by monuments that pour salt in old wounds. The first of these sits at one end of Ledra Street, a major shopping hub in Nicosia. This large piece, designed by the Greek-Cypriot artist Theodoulos Gregoriouis, is titled *Resolution* and depicts angled metal poles driving through the text of the Universal Declaration of Human Rights written in Greek letters. The poles are like shivs stabbed into democracy.

Gregoriouis' work has been featured at the Louvre and the 2004 Athens Olympics and he represented Cyprus at the 2010 Venice Biennale. He often grapples with themes of displacement and identity from the Greek-Cypriot perspective. His ironically-named *Resolution* places the blame for the division of the island squarely on Turkey and Turkish-Cypriots. The Turkish-Cypriots are dehumanized and signified only by long metal poles impaling blocks of Greek text. This negates any ongoing pain felt by Turkish-Cypriots. Displaying the artwork at a porous passport checkpoint between north and south indicates a complete lack of desire to resolve anything between the two sides.

Another sculpture that looms large in the south is a statue of the EOKA fighter Markos Drakos (1930-1957) at the center of a roundabout in Nicosia. There are several monuments to EOKA in the south; their fighters suffered terrible losses at the hands of the British. On the one hand, Drakos died young during the British occupation of Cyprus and can be viewed as a martyr in the fight against colonialism. On the other, EOKA sought *enosis* with Greece and its legacy in the TRNC is a wholly negative one. The EOKA vision for Cyprus did not include Turkish-Cypriots.

Martyrs like Drakos are key figures in Republic of Cyprus' public education program and the concept of martyrdom is at the heart of another piece of public art. The UN buffer zone is meant to be just that: a safe space for Greek and Turkish-Cypriots alike to pass through since the softening of the green line in 2003. However, when you pass from the Greek-Cypriot side of Nicosia into the buffer zone, there is a poster that displays a crowd beating a young man to death. This is the famous image of the death of Tassos Isaac (1972-1996), a Greek-Cypriot man murdered by members of the Turkish paramilitary group called the Grey Wolves. By displaying a poster showing the death of Tassos Isaac at the entrance to the TRNC, the Greek-Cypriot community paints all Turkish-Cypriots with the brush of extremism. (Restrictions on photography within the UN buffer zone prevent the authors from displaying this grotesque image.)

Like the controversial statues of Confederate generals in the American South, these monuments to divisive figures exacerbate painful memories and wounds in Cyprus. They form an integral part of public education in the Republic of Cyprus, which begins in kindergarten and trains children from a young age to fear and loathe their fellow Cypriots across the green line.

Just as public art guides, or dictates, a national narrative about the past so, too, does education.

Dr. Ahmet Sözen, professor of political science and international relations at Eastern Mediterranean University, places the blame for Cyprus' ongoing division squarely at the feet of Cyprus' warring systems of education. He says that "76 percent of Greek-Cypriots rejected the Annan Plan, but 90 percent of young Greek-Cypriots reject it and that is because of the education system."

One would hope that a more modern education system would lead to a greater willingness to reconcile, but this is not the case in Cyprus. In a survey conducted by the authors in January 2020, we found that higher levels of education actually led to less support for a solution: only 44 percent of respondents with a tertiary education level supported a solution compared to 54 percent of respondents with primary or secondary education.

Even back in the period of British rule, the practical challenges of educating Greek and Turkish-Cypriots were profound. The two groups lived in different neighborhoods, spoke different languages, and practiced different faiths. English became the *lingua franca* of education and the British authorities shipped in teachers to work in mixed schools. However, Cypriots already had schools of their own, and most opted to remain ethnically divided. According to Panayiotis Persianis at the University of Cyprus, "the main opposition to these mixed schools came from the Orthodox Church of Cyprus which insisted on continuing its absolute control of Christian/Greek education, which it had during the Turkish rule."[155]

---

155 Panayiotis Persianis, "How have the two separate Education Systems in Cyprus shaped the Perspectives of the Local Communities?," in Iacovos Psaltis et al., eds., *Education in a Divided Cyprus* (Cambridge, UK: Cambridge Scholars Publishing, 2017), 83.

Religion was a core part of the Greek-Cypriot education and the British agreed to this request by creating a Christian Education Board and a Muslim Education Board with the Law of 1895, which allowed religious leaders on both sides to oversee the education of their respective communities. The law allowed for separate religion-based education in Greek and Turkish with textbooks imported directly from Greece and Turkey. Following a Greek-Cypriot uprising in 1933, the British tried to develop a more inclusive and unified form of education, but nationalist rifts had grown far too strong.

These separate education systems were not governed in the same way. The Greek Orthodox Church controlled teacher appointments and syllabi in Greek-Cypriot schools, but the Turkish-Cypriot curriculum was overseen by the British colonial administration and had much less religious influence. These vastly different approaches played a role in Greek-Cypriots rising up against British rule and likewise inspired Turkish-Cypriots to assist the British administration.

Today, in both Greek and Turkish-Cypriot elementary schools, children are inculcated with a belief that their ethnic identity outweighs their nationality. Their respective histories are extensions of Greek and Turkish histories. Greek and Greek-Cypriot children use the same textbooks and share a national education curriculum for elementary school up to grade six. The textbooks glorify the Byzantine Empire and bemoan the Ottoman one as a violent occupying force. Niyazi Kizilyürek, a Turkish-Cypriot scholar and European Parliament MP, notes that Greek and Greek-Cypriot textbooks use the term "Cypriots" (*Kyprioi*) and "Greeks" (*Ellines*) interchangeably and suggest that anyone else who lives on the island is trying to gnaw away at Cypriots' inherently "Hellenic character." Following this logic, Turkish-Cypriots have no claim to equal status in Cypriot society.

These textbooks also feature grisly images of Turks slaughtering Greeks. They demean the Turks as "lazy and greedy" grifters. The books ignore the suffering of Turkish-Cypriots, whom the Greek-Cypriots targeted with systematic violence in the 1960s. They likewise ignore extremist Greek-Cypriot nationalism, while presenting their Turkish-Cypriot counterparts as backward-looking and fanatically religious. For example, in Andreas Polydorou's deeply racist *History of Cyprus*, he writes about the Turkish-Cypriots as Arabs who "had to follow their herds of sheep, and camels and horses in search of food. They lived nomadic lives. That is how most of them live today."[156] By presenting Turkish-Cypriots as stuck in biblical times, Polydorou is part of a larger Greek-Cypriot plan to present Turkish-Cypriots as an impossible future partner. Despite its EU membership, the Republic of Cyprus is unwilling to alter its problematic curriculum to conform to the Council of Europe's inclusive educational goals.

For their part, Turkish-Cypriots have also pushed an ethno-nationalist message through textbooks, most of which were produced during a period of right-wing ascendency in the north. Two of these textbooks were written by the late Vehbi Serter, who was a member of the TRNC's right-wing UBP (National Unity

---

156 Translation and citation of Andreas Polydorou, Istoria tis Kyprou (Nicosia: 1991). Citation in Yiannis Papadakis, "History Education in Divided Cyprus: A Comparison of Greek Cypriot and Turkish Cypriot Schoolbooks on the 'History of Cyprus',"10.

Party). Turkey's twin glories of the Ottoman Empire and Mustafa Kemal Atatürk are at the fore. The books speak of Ottoman prowess on the battlefield and Cyprus' natural connection to Anatolia. The concept "Our Motherland Turkey" is mentioned repeatedly throughout. This is similar to the pro-*Enosis* vantage point of Greek-Cypriot textbooks.

Most crucially, Turkish-Cypriot schoolbooks distinguish between Greeks, whom they call *Yunan* (Ionian) and Greek-Cypriots, whom they call *Rums*, as a means of undercutting the ethnic link that Greeks and Greek-Cypriots like to emphasize. The term *Rum*, derived from "Rome" or the Byzantine Empire, was used during the Ottoman Empire to refer to their Greek Orthodox subjects. Both the Greek-Cypriots and Turkish-Cypriots normalize derogatory terms in their textbooks, teaching generations of children to fear what they don't know.

The two education systems deal with the same events in very different ways. Turkish-Cypriot textbooks highlight the period 1963-74 as a time of systematic mass killing, and use phrases such as "Cyprus is Turkish! The Greek-Cypriot struggle for *enosis* is illegal and barbaric. The EOKA movement is merely a terrorist movement. However, Cyprus is and will remain Turkish."[157] The textbooks also contain images of mass graves. Greek-Cypriots textbooks gloss over the same period. Turkish-Cypriot textbooks celebrate 1974 as a year of liberation; Greek-Cypriot textbooks present 1974 as a year of invasion.

---

157 Vehbi Zeki Serter, "History of the Turkish-Cypriot struggle (1878-1981), vol. 1,61. Cited in Kizilyurek, *National Memory and the Turkish-Cypriot Textbooks*, 393.

There have been recent educational changes in the north. Turkish-Cypriot textbooks underwent a massive change after the 2004 election of the center-left Republican Turkish Party (CTP). Unlike Greek-Cypriot textbooks, which have maintained that the Turkish-Cypriots are inherently Turkish and backwards into the present day, the CTP chose to promote unified "civic nationalism" and hopes for a joint-state. The new textbooks were not afraid of critiquing Turkey; they also remove its "motherland" designation, highlight the divide-and-conquer strategy of Great Britain, and how it exploited differences between the groups. They are also without violent imagery, and they include maps of Cyprus without any dividing lines, promoting the idea that people on both sides are equal Cypriots and deserving of respect. One Turkish-Cypriot textbook features an illustration of an anthropomorphized version of Cyprus that is weeping and grieving; it depicts the island without any divisions, in its "natural state."

Whatever the demerits of the Greek-Cypriot education system, it at least has been effective in encouraging people to vote. The population in the south is politically engaged. Around 80 percent of eligible voters cast ballots in presidential elections.

In the south's most recent presidential elections (2013 and 2018), the conservative President Nicos Anastasiades swept to victory over the liberal AKEL candidate, Stavros Malas. Both of Anastasiades' victories came against the backdrop of significant political headaches: Cyprus' debt crisis of 2012-13 and the failed Crans-Montana peace talks of 2017. In 2013, Anastasiades won with 57 percent of the vote and he claimed his second victory in 2018 with 56 percent. It is notable that the collapse of discussions

with his Turkish-Cypriot counterpart President Mustafa Akıncı
and Cyprus' guarantor powers did not harm his political for-
tunes. Indeed, many of the experts we spoke to explained that
Anastasiades entered the talks at Crans-Montana with his upcom-
ing election front of mind and was not willing to make bold strides
towards a solution because he knew his voters wanted to preserve
the status quo. Thus, a majority of voters in Cyprus have chosen
political candidates who will not end the island's division.

Meanwhile, in the TRNC, President Mustafa Akıncı has long
been an advocate for the reunification of Cyprus. In 2003, he
founded the Peace and Democracy Party to promote reunification
using the model of the Annan Plan. After several unsuccessful bids
for the presidency, he defeated the conservative Derviş Eroğlu in
April 2015 with a definitive 60.5 percent of the vote. His pro-
solution views have made him *persona non grata* in Turkey, and
his criticism of Turkey led President Erdoğan's deputy chairman
Burhan Kuzu to snipe, "If Akıncı likes the Greeks so much, let
him live on the Greek side."[158] While he's never been Ankara's
preferred candidate, it is important to note that Turkish-Cypriot
voters themselves chose a pro-solution president.

Unfortunately, given the TRNC's dependence on Turkey, any
candidate at odds with Ankara cannot hope to last long. In May
2019, Akıncı's coalition government, which brought together
factions from the left, right, and center, collapsed after Ankara
starved it of funds for a year. President Akıncı lost the election in

---

158 Translation courtesy of Google Translate. "Yavru vatan polemigine Kuzu da katildi:
     Sayin Akinci neyine guveniyor anlamadim, " *Haberturk.com*, April 29, 2015.

April 2020, when Ankara supported his opponent, Ersin Tatar, a hard-right candidate. Many observers believe Ankara interfered in the election as some 20,000 more rural voters in Northern Cyprus voted in the second round (and most of these rural voters are settlers from Turkey). Erdoğan had claimed that the Turkish-Cypriot electorate would teach Akıncı "a lesson" by reminding him to "know his limits." The reality of the election, however, wasn't so stark as Erdoğan boasted: Akıncı took 48 percent of the vote. Nevertheless, the election does demonstrate the increasing role that Turkey is playing in the TRNC.

For the most part, Turkish-Cypriots have proven their desire to reunite when they go to the polls. They voted "yes" on the 2004 Annan Plan and they elected Akıncı. Unfortunately, the desires of many are held back both by their complete dependence on Turkey and the obstinance of their Greek-Cypriot counterparts, who are happy with the way things are.

While Cypriot demographics have hindered progress towards a solution, there are a few bright spots that demonstrate the willingness of some Cypriots to move on from the past. Şener Levent, the Turkish-Cypriot editor of the adamantly anti-Erdoğan *Afrika* daily newspaper, was absolved in the TRNC's courts after incensing Ankara by publishing a cartoon of a Greek statue urinating on Erdoğan's head. Levent received an outpouring of support from Cypriots on both sides of the buffer zone. Just a year earlier, a pro-Turkey crowd had thrown stones through *Afrika's* office windows, but the size of that hostile group was nothing compared to the flood of supporters celebrating when Levent and cartoonist Ali Osman Tabak were acquitted, sparing them a possible five-year prison sentence.

In May 2019, Niyazi Kizilyürek became the first Turkish-Cypriot elected in the Republic of Cyprus since 1963. Kizilyürek ran for the European parliament on a pro-reunification platform, and 27.5 percent of Cypriot voters chose him to represent them on the Europe-wide stage.

These are hopeful signs that some Cypriots may be ready to turn a corner, but evidence suggests many will prefer the status quo for a long time to come. The island's most strident voices will likely continue to control the island's political future. This is exacerbated by collapsed peace talks, Turkey's increasing hostility, and the positive reception of status quo presidential candidates in the Republic of Cyprus. If we compound these issues with tensions over settlers in the north and state-mandated education that emphasizes difference and otherness, it's a recipe for more of the same.

CHAPTER 13

Other Obstacles
to a Solution

ERDOĞAN'S PIVOT TO THE EAST, the new Russian influence, and a growing energy conflict would seem to be more than enough challenges to a peaceful resolution of Cyprus's problems. Unfortunately, they are only half of it. Three more factors promising to get in the way are the rise of ethnic nationalism across the globe, the dismantling of the Westphalian compact, and the fact that the TRNC is working well on its own.

Political culture around the globe is moving away from civic nationalism toward ethnic nationalism. Civic nationalists are loyal to the state, whereas ethnic nationalists are loyal to the nation or tribe. Karl Marx believed that all the elements of identity including culture, religion and race would be overtaken by social class. Liberals, too, expected ethnic attachments to weaken over time. This has not been the case. As the political scientist Francis

Fukuyama says: "For the most part, twentieth century politics was defined by economic issues. On the left, politics centered on workers, trade unions, social welfare programs, and redistributive politics. The right, by contrast, was primarily interested in reducing the size of government and promoting the private sector. Politics today, however, is defined less by economics or ideological concerns than by questions of identity."[159]

This politics of identity is destructive and divisive. We are increasingly defined by race, ethnicity, or religion. The seeds were planted in the colonial era when the home countries controlled their colonial subjects by means of divide and rule tactics that were often based on ethnicity. This was certainly the case for the British Empire in Malaysia, India/Pakistan, Kenya, Iraq, Sri Lanka, and Cyprus. Other colonial powers did the same in Syria, Rwanda, the Democratic Republic of Congo, and Lebanon. Today, Fukuyama claims, "The vast majority of the world's nationalist movements do not have a political program beyond the negative desire of independence from some other group or people." As a result, people increasingly define themselves versus the "other."

This has led to ethnic nationalist parties making significant gains in Poland, Hungary, France, Germany, and a number of other European countries. One of the key drivers of the UK's Brexit vote was the fear of immigrants or, more precisely, fear of the unknown: many of the regions that supported Brexit had fewer immigrants than parts of the UK that voted to remain.

---

159 Francis Fukuyama, "The New Tribalism and the Crisis of Democracy," *Foreign Affairs*, September/October 2018.

The United States has also experienced a dramatic tribalist change in a short amount of time. In 2008, the country celebrated the election of its first African-American president. Some eight years later, he was replaced by a man who led the "birther" movement, claiming that Obama had been born in Kenya. Trump was also famously willing to say that there were "fine people on both sides" when confronted with white supremacists marching through the streets of Charlottesville with swastika flags.

This trend is not confined to Europe or North America. Late in 2019, Prime Minister Narendra Modi changed the laws in India so that they would now explicitly favour all immigrants except Muslims. India was once the world's largest secular democracy, but it is now led by a Hindu nationalist. Modi became a hero to the state of Gujarat in 2002 when, as chief minister of the state, he encouraged and was complicit in a Muslim massacre that led to at least 1,000 deaths.

Twenty years ago, this brand of violent ethnic nationalism was universally condemned and attributed mostly to fringe parties. That is no longer the case. Celebrating "political differences" is now encouraged and major governments have validated or excused these ideologies. This emphasis on political difference around the globe will not help Cyprus, where harmful divisions need to be downplayed instead of emphasized.

Cyprus has a stark ethnic divide that can be easily exploited by opportunistic forces. One can see this ethnic divide clearly in a survey conducted in 2008. Some 24 percent of Turkish-Cypriots consider themselves "only or mostly a Turk rather than a Cypriot" while only 20 percent say they are mostly or only a

Cypriot."[160] By contrast, 4 percent of Greek-Cypriots say that they are "only or mostly a Greek rather than a Cypriot" and 41 percent say they are "mostly or only a Cypriot." Greek-Cypriots define themselves as Cypriots (which is a radical change from 60 years ago when they dreamed of joining Greece) and a large portion of Turkish-Cypriots consider themselves to be mostly Turkish. In 2002, Northern Cyprus' founding president Rauf Denktaş told us: "I am Turkish because of my language, my culture, my religion, and my history. I am a Turk who happened to be born in Cyprus."

In 2019, Denktaş' son, Sedar, a current Turkish-Cypriot politician, told us "the Greek Cypriots still think we are the stupid Turks. Many young Greek-Cypriots actually think that we came here after 1974. We have been here for 400 years and for 300 of those years we ruled."

Turk-Cypriots are not alone in emphasizing differences. Greek-Cypriot Archbishop Chrysostomos speaks for many of his fellow citizens when he says, "Cypriot Hellenism is today threatened not just as a nation but also in its religion. This is because the invader is not just of a different race but also of a different religion."[161]

Discussions of who ruled whom, and who "invaded," obscure common ground. It all has to do with ethnic tribalism, says Ingemar Lindahl, "driving people blind and making compromise

---

160 Erol Kaymak, Alexandros Lordos and Nathalie Tocci, *Building Confidence in Peace* (Brussels: Centre for European Policy Studies, 2008), 7.
161 Vassiliou, *From the President's Office*, 253.

impossible. It creates an all or nothing mentality, for which any-thing less is perceived as a betrayal."[162]

Both sides, but especially the Turkish-Cypriots, do not want to live with the other. Some 37 percent of Turkish-Cypriots do not want to have Greek-Cypriots as neighbours; 20 percent of Greek-Cypriots don't want to live next to Turkish-Cypriots.

Historian Thomas Bender, Professor at New York University, believes that a "history in common is fundamental to sustain-ing the affiliation that constitutes national subjects. Nations are, among other things, a collective agreement, partly coerced, to affirm a common history as the basis for a shared future." With this in mind, Greek-Cypriots holding a national holiday to celebrate the victory of Greece over the Ottomans some 200 years ago is unlikely to warm the hearts of their Turkish-Cypriot countrymen.

That ethnic friction has only gotten stronger around the world in the past two decades does not bode well for Cyprus. Dennis Ross, who served as a special advisor to Secretary of State Hillary Clinton, summarizes the ethnic dilemma: "Every state where you have a state that has more than one identity, nation, sector, or tribal—that state is at war with itself. Look at Lebanon, Syria or Iraq. [Put] two national movements . . . together in one state and you will find that one feels the need to dominate the other . . . If you want a prescription for an endless conflict then try to force two national identities into one state."[163]

162 Lindahl, *Notes from the Graveyard*, 110.
163 David Axelrod, Podcast *The Axe Files*, Episode 357, November 25, 2019

Some countries, such as Canada, have been able to meld two or three national identities into one, but these success stories are the exception to the rule. They have stayed united by nurturing minority rights and celebrating compromise even when challenged by extreme elements. For instance, the Pierre Trudeau government required that all candidates for promotion to the rank of colonel had to be bilingual. This was clearly not needed from a military point of view but it was essential to maintaining harmonious relations between the ethnic communities in Canada. In the 2021 federal election all candidates for Prime Minister were able to participate in a two-hour debate in French when four of the five spoke English as their primary language. These are the symbolic gestures that are needed to break ethnic barriers. The majority must go to extra lengths to make the minority feel welcome.

* * *

The 1648 peace of Westphalia brought an end to the Thirty Years' War. Most scholars view the treaty as the very foundation of international relations because it laid out the concept of territorial sovereignty. Essentially, it demanded that any land taken over by military force must be given back to the original nation that owned the territory. This basic premise has been violated numerous times over the centuries but the Westphalian compact has held up fairly well, especially since the end of the Second World War. Israel, despite gaining the Sinai in the 1967 Six Day War, subsequently returned the land to Egypt, its rightful owner. Similarly, the UK went to war to prevent Argentina from keeping the Falkland

Islands, which it had seized by military force. The United States led a multinational coalition to expel Saddam Hussein's Iraqi Army from Kuwait in the First Gulf War, and the Westphalian compact was evoked by the UN and international pundits to demand that Turkey had no right to keep the territory in Cyprus which it had seized during the 1974 invasion. The territory was not returned and Northern Turkey was outlawed.

Three recent violations of the Westphalian compact have weakened the point. The first example is the Turkish attack on the Kurds in Northern Syria in late 2019. The weakened Syrian state could not respond and Erdoğan was given a green light by Trump, who abandoned his Kurdish allies even though they had helped the west in the battle against ISIS.

The second example is the Israeli annexation of the Golan Heights. The Golan Heights were seized by Israel from Syria during the 1967 war. Israel held onto this strategically vital territory for over fifty years but all international observers understood that it would someday be returned to Syria as part of a peace deal. In 2019, the US recognized the Golan Heights as part of Israel, reversing decades of US and International policy. The Fourth Geneva Convention explicitly states that "the occupying power shall not deport or transfer parts of its own civilian population into the territory it occupies." That did not stop Israel or the US.

The last and by far the most serious example of how Westphalian rules have been violated is the Russian invasion and annexation of Crimea in early 2014. It is worth remembering that in a free election, the majority of Ukrainians—both in Crimea and in the Donbas region (which has a high percentage of Russian speakers)—voted for independence from Russia. Russian "green men" and tanks took by force what they had lost at the ballot box. Even if the majority of the population in Crimea had favoured joining Russia, this would still not have given Russia the legal right to take the land by force.

In 1974, when Turkey invaded Cyprus to protect its fellow Turks, there was worldwide condemnation for this aggressive act. The condemnation of Turkey continues forty-eight years later. The international response to Russia's aggression, by contrast, has dissipated quickly. The United States campaigned to allow Russia to keep Crimea and to readmit Russia into the G8 despite its illegal annexation of a sovereign nation's territory. President Trump even defended Russia's seizure of Crimea, claiming that "the people of Crimea, from what I've heard, would rather be with Russia than where they were."

Europe has not stepped up to help Ukraine. The European countries talked tough and imposed economic sanctions on Moscow but did little else. In fact, despite Russia's war of aggression against Ukraine, a majority of delegates to the Parliamentary Assembly of Europe (PACE), including those of Germany, Italy and France, voted in 2019 "to restore the Russian Federation's privileges, apparently all but forgetting the latter's illegal occupation of Ukraine's Crimea."[164] Neither the annexation of Crimea or a pro-Russian faction's shooting down flight MH17, killing 298 innocent passengers and crew members, was enough to encourage

---

164 Alexandra Chyczij, "Remembering the hundreds of innocents Russia murdered five years ago today," *National Post* , July 17, 2019

European governments to stand up to this blatant disregard for Ukraine's rights.

Without international support, the Ukrainians, who lost 13,000 in their fight against Russia, have been forced to negotiate and cede sovereignty to the player with the stronger hand. The Europeans want Russian gas and thus are willing to overlook the fact that Russia engaged in the largest annexation of territory in almost a hundred years.

If Europe is willing to accept Russia's invasion of Crimea, European countries have no moral high ground on which to stand with respect to Turkey's action in Cyprus in 1974 (and we should also remember that Turkey's actions in Cyprus were permitted by a treaty signed by the relevant parties).

These examples clearly demonstrate the increasing disregard for the Westphalian model. The consequences for Cyprus should be obvious. If Russia can keep Crimea and Israel can keep the Golan Heights, why should Turkey give back land to Greek-Cypriots? The Turks have a better historical and political claim to part of Cyprus than do the Russians in Crimea or the Israelis in the Golan Heights. We are not arguing that this is correct or just. Rather, we want to acknowledge that when Turkey's actions in Northern Cyprus are condemned by the global community, that same global community must realize that its own inaction and callow acquiescence in other cases has ripple effects across the globe.

* * *

As for the progress of the Turkish Republic of Northern Cyprus, it is best to step back to 2004. The Greek-Cypriots thought that EU membership would get them get a better deal with Turkey and the Turkish-Cypriots. They placed this bet because they understood Turkey wanted to join the EU and that Cyprus, as a member state, could block Turkey's entrance until it had a deal Greek-Cypriots considered favourable. This bet did not pay, and the prospect for Turkey's entry into the EU is now remote.

The Greek-Cypriots also gambled that the economic and political situation would get worse for the Turkish-Cypriots. This has not happened. Former TNRC cabinet minister and current Democrat Party MP Sedar Denktaş asserts that the Turkish-Cypriots are doing quite well and experiencing financial growth. He claimed that "in 1974 our [Turkish-Cypriot] per capita income was US$500 and the Greek-Cypriots had a per capita income of US$5,000. Now we in the north have US$14,000 and the Greek-Cypriots are at US$25,000." Thus, according to him, the Turkish-Cypriots have closed the gap. World Bank economic data is scarce but what is available would suggest that Greek-Cypriots GNP per capita is two times that of the Turkish-Cypriot community and that with purchasing power parity, the per capita income in the south may only be 35 percent higher than the north. This would support Denktaş's claim.

The TRNC was able to close this gap. largely due to heavy financial support from Turkey. It is impressive progress. The Turkish-Cypriots may not have achieved parity, but they are gaining and their standard of living is considerably better today that it was in 1974.

The TRNC has also proven that, despite its isolation, it can function as a community and a working democracy. Free and fair elections have been held and once the patriarch Rauf Denktaş was out of office, the competing parties have alternated in power. There is a functioning government in place, one that did not exist in 1974 and was not fully baked in 2004. It will be difficult for the Turkish-Cypriot elites now to give up power and revert to being a minority and possibly second-class citizens in a larger Cyprus. "The Turkish-Cypriots are fine with the status quo," writes Robert MacDonald in *The Problem with Cyprus*. "They have now had too long being their own master with their own courts, own education, own government, and own police." This is why the only workable solution for a united Cyprus is one where the two ethnic states retain much of their original power to govern their own constituents.

Of all the factors we have noted that have changed since 2004—Erdrogan's shift, Russian influence, demographics, ethnic nationalism, the decline of the Westphalian compact, the success of the TRNC, and natural gas—only the last has the potential to bring the sides closer together rather than dividing them further and, as we saw, energy riches are far from a sure thing. The failure of the Greek-Cypriot elites to capitalize on the opportunity of 2004 looks worse as time passes. The two sides continue to talk, but these talks have gone on for over forty-eight years and we are no closer to a solution today than we were in the 1970s. We need a radically new approach.

PART IV

Where Do We Go From Here?

"Compromise does not mean cowardice: indeed it is frequently the compromisers and conciliators who are faced with the severest tests of political courage as they oppose the extremist views of their constituents"

JOHN F. KENNEDY, *PROFILES IN COURAGE*

CHAPTER 14

Where We Stand Today

TEN YEARS AGO, Robert Rotberg said that the "biggest obstacle to a negotiated settlement of outstanding differences [in Cyprus]—to the acceptance of a reconfigured Annan Plan or something better—is that the status quo works and has long worked, especially for south Cyprus. Few shots are fired across the green line; UN soldiers and monitors have little to do except to watch Cypriots and tourists cross the green line in both directions."[165]

A Canadian diplomat echoed these sentiments: "For Greek-Cypriots, the irony is that life is pretty good. The financial crisis in 2008 scared them but now they have a Greek Orthodox state and don't need to compromise with Turkish-Cypriots in their government."

---

165 Robert Rothberg, "Reunifying Cyprus: Essential Challenges," in *Reunifying Cyprus The Annan Plan and Beyond*, eds. Andrekos Varnova and Hubert Faustmann (London: I. B. Tauris, 2009), 246.

A recent survey shows that while both sides are unhappy with the political situation in Cyprus, the Greek-Cypriots are fairly happy with their lives: 51 percent of Greek-Cypriots say they are satisfied and only 3 percent say they are dissatisfied.[166] Only 29 percent of Turkish-Cypriots say they are satisfied with their lives but on the whole they, too, are comfortable as things stand.

We asked all the Cyprus experts that we interviewed over the past few years, including academics, politicians, and diplomats, where they thought Cyprus would be a decade from now. Some of these experts were Greek or Greek-Cypriot, some were Turkish-Cypriot, and some were foreigners not affiliated with either side in this dispute. We asked them to choose from four possible outcomes: the current status quo would prevail; a bi-zonal, bi-communal deal would be reached (based on something similar to the Annan Plan); two independent states would be recognized on the island; Cyprus would be joined as one unitary state.

The results are astonishing, unambiguous, and pessimistic. Almost half the individuals who closely follow this issue believe that nothing will change and the situation today will be exactly the same even ten years from now. Partition will continue. All particularly agree that a unitary state (the dream of many Greek-Cypriots) is very unlikely to be the outcome.

If we look at a more detailed breakdown of the experts' views, we find differences based on their affiliation and background. The Greek or Greek-Cypriot experts and politicians we interviewed are

166 Kaymak, Lordos and Tocci, *Building Confidence in Peace*, 13.

the most optimistic. They believe (or at least told us they believe) that the most likely outcome ten years from now would be one BZBC nation under something similar to the Annan Plan. Fully 53 percent of Greek-Cypriot experts believe this, while only one in four think the status quo will prevail. They do not believe the island will still be partitioned in ten years.

By contrast, more than half (53 percent) of the foreign experts, diplomats and politicians we interviewed—none of them affiliated with either the Greek-Cypriots or the Turkish-Cypriots—believe the status quo will prevail. These realists have watched round after round of negotiations go nowhere. Virtually the same percentage of this non-affiliated group believe that either there will be a two-state solution (21 percent) or that both sides will be one nation under a BZBC arrangement (23 percent).

The most pessimistic group by far are the Turkish-Cypriots, with two-thirds believing that the status quo will be the most likely outcome ten years from now. Ozdil Nami told us he feels "the political landscape in the north will change dramatically in ten years. The Turkish-Cypriots will not be as influential and the north will be less inclined to live with Greek-Cypriots."

Both sides blame each other but both agree on where this is heading if they do not find a solution. What will happen to the Turkish-Cypriots if a solution isn't reached? They ultimately are in danger of extinction. Turkey is moving in and staking its claim; as Ahmet Sozen told us when we met in the Buffer Zone in Nicosia, "over time the TRNC will *de facto* be a province of Turkey. This is not good for Turkish-Cypriots but in the long run it is not good for Greek-Cypriots either." Turkish-Cypriots may not see themselves as part of a province of Turkey, but this is what will happen as more Turks emigrate to the TRNC and young Turkish-Cypriots head for greener pastures elsewhere in the world.

In January 2020, we commissioned a survey of five-hundred Greek-Cypriots; our goal was to understand where the Greek-Cypriot voters (as opposed to their experts) stood with respect to a solution. We chose to focus on Greek-Cypriots because they are the voting bloc on the island most strongly opposed to a basic BZBC federation. The concept of a BZBC federation is the basis for any possible reconciliation deal, and if the Greek-Cypriots don't agree to it, then it is highly unlikely.

The survey showed that only 48 percent of Greek-Cypriots would vote "yes" for a BZBC federation. This is identical to the 48 percent that said the same in a December 2018 World Bank survey. We didn't survey Turkish-Cypriots for this 2020 report, but that earlier World Bank survey found that 59 percent of Turkish-Cypriots would vote "yes" in a referendum. This validates our position that the Greek-Cypriots continue to be the negative factor with respect to getting to a successful referendum result.

The 48 percent Greek-Cypriot support for a BZBC federation is significantly higher than the percentage that voted for the Annan Plan back in 2004. But this percentage is certainly inflated by many of the Greek-Cypriots who would only vote "yes" on the assumption that the BZBC deal offered would address all of their concerns and thus be acceptable to them. This sort of deal would be one-sided and would lead to Turkish-Cypriot rejection in a referendum. When an actual deal is presented, as with the Annan Plan, then the Greek-Cypriots will most likely again be negative about many of the details and this 48 percent "yes" vote would shrink.

The survey's responses to specific issues demonstrate that getting to a workable solution will be virtually impossible. Let's look at just three of the key issues for Greek-Cypriots. When presented with the statement that "the property issue should be resolved primarily through restitution", 78 percent of Greek-Cypriots said this was either desirable or essential. But restitution is never going to be part of any compromise BZBC deal. A workable deal that will be acceptable to the Turkish-Cypriots will handle property on the basis of compensation rather than restitution. This is the problem with asking if Greek-Cypriots are in favour of a BZBC federation without specifying the nature of the deal.

Another 56 percent of Greek-Cypriots say that "Cyprus should be fully demilitarized following a solution, with the withdrawal of foreign military units and the dissolution of local military units." Again, this is unlikely to happen at the level or pace that will help the Greek-Cypriots to think it will be acceptable for them to vote "yes" for a BZBC federation.

Finally, only 20 percent of Greek-Cypriots agree that "under a solution, all or almost all Greek-Cypriots should live in the Greek-Cypriot state and all or almost all Turkish-Cypriots should live in the Turkish-Cypriot state." This, however, is contemplated in a BZBC federation as understood by Turkish-Cypriots, and it is exactly what the Annan Plan proposed. There will be no deal if the result is that the Turkish-Cypriots will be overwhelmed in the north by Greek-Cypriots, making them the minority in their own state within the new Cyprus.

Back in 2009, editors Andrekos Varnava and Hubert Faustmann published *Reunifying Cyprus: The Annan Plan and Beyond*. It was an excellent post-mortem of the Annan Plan and why it failed, and it pointed out five changes that were deemed essential by at least 70 percent of Greek-Cypriots in order to incline them to support a BZBC plan. Those five changes deemed essential in order of importance were the withdrawal of Turkish troops at a faster pace than provided for in the UN Plan; Turkey to compensate Greek-Cypriot refugees who will not be getting their property back; more Turkish immigrants to leave the island than was provided for in the UN Plan; the cost of the federal state to be divided more equitably so that Greek-Cypriots do not end up shouldering 90 percent of the cost; international guarantees for the implementation of the solution with serious consequences for the side that breaks from the agreed terms.

It is highly unlikely that any new compromise deal will address these five issues, even though a majority of Greek-Cypriots deem them to be essential.

If these issues are essential to a deal but will never happen, does that mean we'll never get a deal? Fortunately, the search for a workable solution continues despite the many forces working against it. The last concerted effort to move forward was held at Crans-Montana in Switzerland in late 2017. The UN sponsored talks were monitored by Espen Barth Eide, the UN secretary-general's special advisor on Cyprus. Unfortunately, like so many negotiations that preceded it, ten days of intense discussions went nowhere.

The reasons for the failure are no different from the reasons for the collapse of the Annan Plan thirteen years earlier. The same issues have divided and will continue to divide the two sides. Every expert knows this. The UN knows this but cannot say so publicly. Several observers told us that the UN's own surveys and analysis confirm this view but that it would be politically incorrect for any UN spokesperson to articulate this truth.

These areas of disagreement are fundamental issues of principle. Greek-Cypriots want a truly independent sovereign nation without any foreign interference; Turkish-Cypriots would prefer to have some protection provided by the Turkish Army along with Turkish guarantees. Greek-Cypriots want a Greek-Cypriot state with a protected Turkish-Cypriot minority; Turkish-Cypriots want to be partners. Greek-Cypriots want a democratic state that, like other nations, relies on a "one-person one-vote" system; Turkish-Cypriots want promised safeguards to their minority rights (which they had in the 1960 constitution). These have been the fundamental obstacles since 1974. Neither side is willing to back down on principle, making compromise impossible.

Following the breakdown of the Crans-Montana talks, both sides blamed the other for the impasse. The international consensus is that it was the Greek-Cypriots who were not prepared or willing to negotiate. Ahmet Sozen told us that "Anastasiades was aware of the deal he was going to get and he would not be able to sell it to the Greek-Cypriot community. If there was no requirement for a referendum, he might have accepted." Lord Hannay further corroborated this opinion, stating that everyone he's spoken to believes it was "the Greek-Cypriots who were completely at fault at Crans-Montana. The Turks made bigger security concessions but Anastasiades decided that getting re-elected was more important than getting to a solution."

In fact, Anastasiades was surprised that Turkey and the Turkish-Cypriots were so willing to make concessions when he had hoped simply for discussions that would lead to more discussions. It is also possible that Turkey and the Turkish-Cypriots were willing to offer concessions because they knew Anastasiades' strategy and were confident that he would never accept what was on offer. We might never know. At this point, it seems clear that the Greek-Cypriot preferred outcome is either getting much more than they have been offered or keeping the status quo.

The Greek-Cypriots will continue to stall and watch as talks go nowhere, anxious to appear a willing partner but never giving in on the core demands that the Turkish-Cypriots require to get to "yes." The fundamental truth, then, is that the Greek-Cypriot people do not want a bi-zonal, bi-communal confederation of two nations within one state. This is unacceptable to a super-majority of Greek-Cypriots. Anastasiades may be stalling, but he is ultimately listening to his constituents. Short of finding a charismatic Greek-Cypriot leader who can share a compelling vision for a united Cyprus, there is little hope for a solution based on the same framework that has been failing miserably since 1974.

Post Crans-Montana, Cyprus, if anything, has regressed. "I would say that today we see more movement backwards than forwards," says Lord Hannay. One UN person admitted to us "there is deal fatigue. People feel burned." In order to regain momentum for a solution, Cyprus needs to deviate from the past and take the risk of a new way forward. UN Secretary General Guterres said that "new ideas" may be needed to get to a settlement. We couldn't agree more.

CHAPTER 15

The Way Forward

THE PATH OF LEAST RESISTANCE in Cyprus is maintaining the status quo. Standing firm means that no one has to take political risks, and there is also the fact that Cyprus is relatively peaceful today. There is no urgent need for expediency. Kamel Vicari, a Unite Cyprus Now activist, rightfully points out: "There are so many other problems in the world. We Cypriots are very spoiled thinking we are the only problem on the planet, that everybody should pay attention to us. They will not, we need to sit down and sort out our mess."[167]

Left to their own devices, the people of Cyprus will get nowhere. A 2015 study found that 70 percent of people on the island support a solution but only 15-20 percent believe one will happen. Every attempt at a resolution for the past sixty years has required

---

167 Kamel Vicari, *Cyprus News Digest* Podcast, July 12, 2019.

the active intervention of a third party. "Without outside prod-
ding," says Erol Kaymak, "there is no way to get a solution."[168]

One outside force that could light a fire under both protagonists
is the UN. It could simply give Cyprus six-months' notice that
the UNFICYP peacekeeping troops will be withdrawn. This could
easily be accomplished: the entire Security Council is not required
to agree. However, when we mentioned this idea to UN officials,
they were uniformly opposed. They feel the objective of "first do
no harm" means that the UN should stay in Cyprus indefinitely
(forever, if required). They believe they are saving lives, which is
historically true, and that there is potential for turmoil if the UN
leaves Cyprus.

At the same time, UN officials admit they are a roadblock to a
solution, particularly in the Greek part of the island. The Turkish-
Cypriots do not need or want the UN Forces, because they are
protected by the Turkish Army. The Greek-Cypriots desperately
want the UN troops to stay and already pay a significant portion
of the UNFICYP costs. In the 2020 survey that we conducted,
46 percent of Greek-Cypriots said they would be less likely to
vote "yes" for a BZBC federation if the UN withdrew its troops,
compared to 27 percent who said that it would make them more
likely to vote "yes." But we strongly believe that the opposite would
happen.

If UN peacekeeper withdrawal was a reality and not just a hypo-
thetical posed in a survey question, Greek-Cypriot minds would

---

168 Erol Kaymak, "Adopting a Piecemeal Approach," in *Resolving Cyprus*, ed. James
Ker-Lindsay (London: I.B. Tauris, 2016), 138.

concentrate on the need to get to a permanent resolution of some sort. The UN serves as a security blanket for Greek-Cypriots: removing it is the only way to make sure that they come to the negotiating table with a willingness to compromise.

Both sides would also benefit from a short timeline for striking a deal, ideally six months. "For any future negotiations," says Özdil Nami, "both sides must agree up front on a finite time for discussions (months not years) and if at the end of that period there are still outstanding issues then both sides must give the UN the role of arbitrator and vote on the proposed deal." This would prevent negotiations from dragging on endlessly through multiple rounds as they have in the past.

Finally, the negotiations would follow a two-phase program designed to lead only to a resolution. The first phase would be to build on the BZBC proposals that formed the basis of both the Annan Plan and the more recent negotiations at Crans-Montana. If the first phase of negotiations failed or wound up rejected by either the Greek-Cypriots or Turkish-Cypriots in a referendum, the negotiations would move to a second phase where each side would agree on the terms of a "velvet" divorce.

This last step is essential. The Greek-Cypriots need to understand that if there is another referendum, and it fails to pass, international recognition of the TRNC will be inevitable. There is no going back to the status quo. This should give the Greek-Cypriots the motivation they need to engage seriously in talks. As the Annan Plan itself corroborated, a breakdown of talks followed by "secession of a sovereign Turkish-Cypriot state and the consequent partition of Cyprus could be described as the Greek-Cypriot nightmare."[169] The Turkish-Cypriots, too, would be motivated. The current situation where, as the Annan plan noted, "the larger Greek-Cypriot population alone exercising the sovereignty of the state could be described as the Turkish-Cypriot nightmare." Neither side is likely to be entirely happy with the terms of either a BZBC deal or a divorce, but each has a legitimate chance to find a resolution that is better than worst-case.

Let's review the elements of each phase. Getting to a bi-zonal, bi-communal agreement similar to the Annan plan will be more difficult than it was in 2004, when the Greek-Cypriots rejected it and Turkish-Cypriots voted in favor. As noted earlier, the world has changed: the TRNC is now a functional government with a growing economy; Turkey and Russia have more influence on the island, and the EU is a less attractive club than it was two decades ago. A Turkish-Cypriot "yes" vote is no longer a given. Both sides will have to commit to the process and compromise.

The first key yet contentious issue will be political equality. The Turkish-Cypriots were effectively given this in the 1960 constitution by virtue of their political representation and their vetoes. Greek-Cypriots have never been comfortable with these grants, and unilaterally withdrew the minority rights of Turkish-Cypriots in 1963.

Greek-Cypriots point to their Hellenic and democratic roots, and a lot of contemporary political philosophy that says the majority should prevail, and that minorities receive only those protections that the majority determines they deserve. Of course, other schools

169 Kofi Annan, "Report on Good Offices in Cyprus," *United Nations Document*, April 1, 2003.

of political philosophy hold that even within a majoritarian system, minorities should possess equal rights, protected by equal law, in order to avoid oppression. Canada, again, has accorded minority rights to French-Canadians and these rights have been instrumental in preserving unity in the country.

Let's be clear: there is no deal possible in Cyprus unless there is political equality and preservation of adequate minority rights for Turkish-Cypriots in a newly unified Cyprus.

Another issue that will be non-negotiable for the Turkish-Cypriots is the question of property rights and the prospect of having their own state. Lost Greek-Cypriot property in the north will have to be addressed by compensation, as was outlined in the Annan Plan, rather than by restitution, which is what the Greek-Cypriots would prefer. As the surveys clearly indicate, any reversal of this policy will never be accepted by the Turkish-Cypriots. Allowing unlimited return of Greek-Cypriots to their former properties in the north would mean that the Turkish-Cypriots would eventually be a minority even in their own state.

There are many international precedents for limits on the return of Greek-Cypriots to the north. For example, based on Article 35A of the Indian Constitution, Indians were not able to buy land in Kashmir. This was meant to protect seven million mostly Muslim Kashmiri from being overwhelmed by 1.3 billion Indians. India recently reversed this ruling, but the restrictions held for many years. Turkish-Cypriots will have to be reassured that they will be master in their own house. In Canada, the French-Canadians similarly want to be *"Maitres chez nous"* in the French-Canadian province of Quebec. This Turkish-Cypriot demand to protect their majority in their own state within a united Cyprus is a reasonable request to protect minority rights in a new federation.

Our own studies and surveys conducted by the World Bank and European Union in 2018 indicate that the above terms would be central to getting the Turkish-Cypriots to agreement. For sake of simplicity, let us assume this is a deal that could be reached and would be supported by both the Turkish-Cypriots and Turkey. What about the Greek-Cypriots?

Any agreed solution will need to be more compelling to Greek-Cypriots than the Annan Plan was in 2004. We suggest three changes that might help bring them to "yes." First and most important, a deal will need to address security. Security was, and is, important to both communities but it is a deal breaker for the Greek-Cypriots, who genuinely and reasonably fear the Turkish Army; many lived through the 1974 invasion. In our 2020 survey, women were much less supportive of voting "yes" in a referendum for a BZBC Federation, and a significant driver of this position was security. In polls following the 2005 referendum, a majority of Greek-Cypriots (61.9 percent) said they would support Annan Plan with better security guarantees.[170]

Greek-Cypriot concerns about security can be addressed by establishing a faster and more significant withdrawal of Turkish Troops from Cyprus, as was tentatively agreed upon at Crans-Montana by the Turks and Turkish-Cypriots.

---

170 Neophytos Loizides, "Pro: An Appraisal of the Functionality of Annan VI," in *Reunifying Cyprus*, eds. Andrekos varnava and Hubert Faustmann (London: I. B. Tauris, 2009), 80.

A second change that would help Greek-Cypriots accept a settlement would be to remove the British military from Cyprus entirely. Under the Annan Plan, the Brits were willing to return to Cyprus one of their two military sovereign base areas on the island. In order to make the new deal more attractive to Greek-Cypriots, the British should give back both bases and cede the entire 98.1 square miles of land that they occupy on Cypriot soil.

The Cypriots would be glad to see the bases gone. Christopher Hitchens noted, these British bases have been a source of trouble and tension, and a "constant temptation to outsiders to treat Cyprus as a tactical or strategic pawn rather than as a country with a complex individuality."[171]

Such a withdrawal would meet with considerable resistance in the UK; the bases have been important to Britain, and will only become more important in the future. Many believe that given the turbulence in the Middle East, the threat of ISIS, and the value of communications intelligence, the bases are now more valuable to Britain and the West than they have ever been. One senior former British diplomat told us that Prime Minister Gordon Brown had been willing to give up the bases but that "the deep state in the UK is very much in favour of keeping the bases."

That may be true, but Cyprus is a sovereign country and we would argue that the bases are an affront to Cypriot legitimacy and an unfortunate remnant of Britain's colonial past. In any court of international justice, the UK would lose the right to maintain

171 Hitchens, *Hostage to History*, 163.

these sovereign base areas. The Chagos Island case in Mauritius is an illustrative precedent. The UK kept its base on Chagos when Mauritius was granted independence from Britain in 1968. The International Court of Justice in February 2019 called on Britain to relinquish the territory to Mauritius. Despite heavy lobbying by both the UK and the US (which uses the base and values its strategic importance), the UN Grand Assembly voted 116 to 6 in favour of the base being returned to Mauritius. The case of the British bases in Cyprus is no different. Indeed, the attorney-general of Cyprus has argued that the Mauritius ruling opens up the possibility of Cyprus legally forcing the UK to close its bases.

If the British returned both bases, the Greek-Cypriots could redevelop one of them and then potentially rent the other base to the European Union. This move would have great economic consequences and an even greater security impact. The Greek-Cypriots do not trust the British to protect them from the Turks—especially given that the Brits stood by in 1974 when Turkey invaded Cyprus. They would, however, welcome EU protectors, because they are EU members. Even more importantly, the British exit from Cyprus would be a huge psychological win for the Greek-Cypriots, throwing off the cloak of the former colonial power.

The third change necessary for Greek-Cypriots to accept a deal is courageous and effective Greek-Cypriot leadership. The Greek-Cypriots did not have strong leadership with Papadopoulos in 2004 or with Anastasiades at Crans-Montana in 2018. Indeed, they have been ill-served by all of their leaders, short of Vassiliou. Lord Hannay claims that the "Greek-Cypriots have been fed a diet of lies by their political leaders. The leaders refuse to tell them the truth: that they will not get everything they want."

The Greek-Cypriot leaders have not prepared the population to accept the compromises that they will need to make to get a deal done. They have led their people to believe that the Turkish-Cypriots will compromise on all matters that are important to Greek-Cypriots, including security guarantees, departures of settlers, and the right to return to their former homes in the north. These compromises were unacceptable in 2004 and they are even more unacceptable to Turkey and the Turkish-Cypriots today, given how the strategic landscape has changed.

We ran up against the fact that many Greek-Cypriots today are unaware of the key elements of BZBC when we began discussing with pollsters the survey we wished to undertake for this book. One firm we interviewed pushed back on our line of questioning, insisting that most Greek-Cypriots did not have enough knowledge of the elements of the BZBC concept, as represented by either the Annan Plan or Crans-Montana, to answer accurately our questions. To the extent that this is true, it is a failure of the Greek-Cypriot leadership. Anastasiades or his successor needs either to lead Greek-Cypriots to a deal, impressing upon them that their negotiating hand has deteriorated since 2004 and will only get weaker in the future, or explicitly admit that no BZBC framework will be acceptable to the majority of Greek-Cypriots.

If, under the terms we've discussed, the two sides are unable to come to an agreement that can be put to a referendum, they should go their separate ways. This move may seem dramatic but after close to six decades of acrimony surely it is time to move on. As the *Economist* correctly pointed out:

> Breaking up a country should never be done lightly, because it is a painful process—politically, economically and emotionally. Ask the Indians, Pakistanis and Bangadeshis or the Serbs, Croats and other former citizens of Yugoslavia. Few splits happen as peaceably as that of the Czechs and Slovaks.[172]

But this last resort will probably be necessary. Even with the improvements that we have suggested above, we believe it is unlikely that the two sides will agree to a compromise that brings them back together. There is too much history, too many years of misinformation on both sides, and too much mistrust to give us confidence in a deal. In a survey of a thousand Cypriots, 72 percent of Turkish-Cypriots said they do not trust Greek-Cypriots, and 39 percent of Greek-Cypriots do not trust Turkish-Cypriots.[173] These scars may never heal. The core challenge, says a Canadian diplomat, is that most Greek-Cypriots have never met a Turkish-Cypriot, and vice versa.

If we can bridge this gap in trust, divorce would be the next best thing to a BZBC resolution. As happened in Czechoslovakia in 1993, a "velvet divorce"—a peaceful, smooth transition into two equal halves—would bring stability, peace, increased tourism, and a return of land and economic compensation for lost property.

---

172 "The Untied Kingdom," *Economist*, April 17, 2021, 17.
173 Kaymak, Lordos and Tocci, *Building Confidence in Peace*, 24-25.

Unfortunately, in the January 2020 survey that we conducted it is clear that a velvet divorce is not supported by Greek-Cypriots. In fact, 47 percent of them either strongly oppose or oppose a velvet divorce while only 31 percent strongly support or support the idea. Again, most don't want to share a divided island with a sovereign Turkish-Cypriot state. But that matters less to younger Greek-Cypriots. Some 45 percent of those under 35 support a divorce compared to 32 percent of those over 55 years old. This demonstrates the level of distrust among younger Greek-Cypriots, who have never interacted or lived with Turkish-Cypriots.

The younger Greek-Cypriots want to get on with life. They enjoy their lives in relative tranquility and prosperity. If the idea of a BZBC federation can't be attained, the Greek-Cypriot political leadership should help the country come to terms with the fact that, in the long run, a velvet divorce is comprehensively better than the status quo.

If both parties agree to the provisions of the velvet divorce, it is easy to see how the TRNC will benefit. The TRNC would be independent and would be recognized by the world community. Why would or should the Greek-Cypriots agree to this arrangement? We would argue that they would benefit, first and foremost, from the certainty it would bring to an island that has faced chaos, disruption, and turmoil for over sixty years. The economic benefits would be enormous. Business abhors uncertainty, and an agreed solution would lead to dramatic increases in investment and tourism on the entire island. Cyprus is a gem, but the island is unable to exploit its many advantages because of the tension caused by the de facto wall separating north and south and the ongoing presence of UN blue helmets.

The south also could see other great economic benefits from a relationship with the north. Prior to 1974, fully two-thirds of tourism, two-thirds of cultivated land, and 60 percent of mining and quarrying was on territory that is now part of the Turkish-Cypriot north.[174] A May 2014 study by PRIO Cyprus Centre suggests that annual growth could be 2.8 percent higher for twenty years with a settlement; that would add US $15,000 to average incomes in Cyprus.[175] Eventually, years of peace between these two sovereign nations would lead to more open borders and a friendly co-existence, which the island has not known for over sixty years.

Greek-Cypriots would also get 7 to 8 percent of their land back (as per the Annan Plan) and those unable to return to their properties in the north would be given financial compensation. The international community would need to participate in this compensation given the state of the economy in Northern Cyprus. Greek-Cypriots could see off the British and recover one of their two bases, with the other becoming an EU base which would provide much-wanted security while also giving the West a valuable strategic outpost in the Eastern Mediterranean. Both sides would be able to import power from Turkey, which would reduce their costs to a quarter of what they currently pay.

Finally, a peaceful separation would also lead to the maximization of the economic potential of the Cyprus gas reserves. The uncertainty would disappear and the optimal route for the pipeline via Turkey would be used to get the gas to market. Fiona Mullen of

174 Hitchens, *Hostage to History*, 104-105.
175 "The Cyprus Problem: Intractable or Insoluble, " *Economist*, November 29, 2014, 49.

Sapienta Economics says that "laying a gas pipeline from Cyprus to Turkey would be $15 billion cheaper than the $20 billion alternative of building a liquefied natural gas plant."[176] This economic link with Turkey would also serve to lessen tensions between Cyprus and Turkey; both sides would benefit from exploitation of the gas reserves.

It would be wise, in the event of a divorce, for Greek-Cypriot leadership to lobby to have the newly recognized TRNC in the EU. That would mean that both parts of Cyprus would be EU members and there would be no hard border on the island. (As of right now, our 2020 survey indicates Greek-Cypriots would prefer not to have the TRNC join the EU as a separate state. We suspect the answer would be different if the TRNC were a sovereign and recognized nation.)

Whether a newly established TRNC were admitted to the EU or not, we would argue that separation is still better for Greek-Cypriots than the status quo. Greek-Cypriots have been led down a path by leaders promising that a better deal can be had tomorrow. Palestinian leaders have done the same since 1948. They all have been proven wrong with the passage of time.

We've focused our attention on how Greek-Cypriots would benefit from this divorce, because they have shown the strongest resistance. If nothing happens, the continuation of the status quo will calcify and the Greek-Cypriots will wind up sharing a hard border with arch-enemy Turkey rather than an almost invisible border with their fellow Cypriots.

---

176 "The Future of Cyprus: a troubled story," Economist, March 30, 2013, 49.

CHAPTER 16

Conclusion

W E BEGAN THIS BOOK recounting the tremendous affection that we have for Cyprus and for both Greek-Cypriots and Turkish-Cypriots. Cyprus is one of the world's most beautiful and historic islands. Its people are proud descendants of the Hellenic and Ottoman traditions. They deserve to have their issues resolved and to fully and peacefully achieve their enormous potentials.

The fact that the island is small and not at war, or as volatile as many other parts of the Middle East, has left the international community to focus on larger problems. "Cyprus is the best candidate to achieve peace in the world," former Turkish-Cypriot cabinet minister Ozdil Nami told us, "but for the UN, unless there is a big crisis, they don't need to act. This means that when there *is* a crisis, they can't react."

It is time for Cypriots themselves to lead this process. After all these years of trying, it is certainly worth one last attempt to see if a reunification deal is possible. Getting a deal done will require compromise on both sides. History does not give us much confidence that this next attempt will turn out any differently from the previous efforts, but it is the best possible outcome and it deserves one last chance.

A close look at the survey we conducted in 2020 shows that the strong Greek-Cypriot preference is for a reunited Cyprus as a unitary state where everyone gets one vote. Over 76 percent of Greek-Cypriots rated this as a 4 or a 5 on desirability scale, where 5 is the highly desirable. By contrast, only 38 percent rated a BZBC Federation solution as desirable and close to the same percentage (34 percent) rated this as not very desirable. The other alternatives were viewed even less favourably, including the status quo (69 percent undesirable, and the two versions of a velvet divorce, which were rated lowest of all five alternative scenarios. The option of northern Cyprus being a province of Turkey is clearly the worst outcome for Greek-Cypriots and yet this is exactly where non-action and the status quo is likely to lead.

When asked which of these five outcomes that they see as most likely 10 years from now, the picture changes radically and in some ways mirrors what we saw from our survey of experts, although ordinary Greek-Cypriots are much more pessimistic than the Greek and Greek-Cypriot experts we discussed in the previous chapter. The Greek-Cypriots respond that the status quo will still prevail, with some 67 percent rating this very likely or likely (versus the 26% of the Greek and Greek-Cypriot experts we interviewed). All three main Greek-Cypriot political parties are essentially in favour of the status quo so there is no impetus for change. The next most likely outcome is a BZBC solution but only 21 percent of Greek-Cypriots see this as likely. Looking at these numbers should give us all pause as to the probability of any BZBC deal; the Greek-Cypriots have been down this path many times before. The other three alternatives are seen as even more unlikely.

Unfortunately, the outcome that the Greek-Cypriots most prefer, a unitary state, is also one that they realize is not likely. When you put the Greek-Cypriot preference for each of the five outcomes together with their view of the likelihood of each, it is clear that no outcome is both preferable and likely. The most likely outcome is status quo, and that is only the third best possible outcome. The velvet divorce, which we recommend, is viewed as a negative and improbable outcome by Greek-Cypriots.

Asked to choose between only two available options, a BZBC Federation or a permanent division of the Island, the majority of Greek-Cypriots (56 percent) chose a BZBC Federation and only 27 percent chose division. That would seem to offer hope for the future, but remember what we have said about theoretically asking Greek-Cypriots this question: they choose BZBC without understanding the compromises necessary to get a deal done. In practice, they have consistently shown that they reject the essential elements of a BZBC deal. Greek-Cypriots have been masters in their own house for over fifty years and they have no intention of sharing power again. Their leaders, meanwhile, obdurately refuse to admit that their preferred version of BZBC is unacceptable to Turkish-Cypriots.

The two communities, but most specifically the Greek-Cypriot side, think they hold a winning hand and that time will ensure that their hand only gets better. Both sides, and particularly the

Greek-Cypriots, are deluding themselves, and that is nothing new. Rita Severis wrote a book chronicling 250 years of artists travelling through Cyprus. In her final chapter, she says that "obstinacy and immaturity in political affairs led the Greek-Cypriots into unforeseen situations and often prevented them from choosing easier, although potentially long term and successful methods of pursuing their aims." The Greek-Cypriot hand did not get better over the last eighteen years. They are now faced with a more confident Turkish-Cyprus, and a stronger Turkey than was the case eighteen years ago. The EU, moreover, has far less to offer the Turkish parties to leverage a deal.

Vassiliou was the only Cypriot President farsighted enough to understand that compromise is the way to pursue successful long-term aims. In his book *From the President's Office*, he wrote:

> The national tragedy of Cyprus is unfortunately due to the fact that many of its political leaders have never accepted or recognized reality and the need, for instance, to abandon early on the concept of *Enosis* and embrace the treaties of Zurich and London; to accept, after the numerous mistakes and crimes associated with the coup and the invasion, the compromise that Makarios was obliged, as things developed, to subscribe to in accepting the bi-zonal, bi-communal federation. These people did not realize the need for such a compromise so that we can build a new Cyprus, a unified Cyprus which will not be a problem within a united Europe.[177]

---

177 Vassiliou, *From the President's Office*, 260.

Egos and political realities, especially in the south, mean that compromise is effectively political suicide. Perhaps the Greek-Cypriots could learn from the North Macedonians, who put their egos aside to get to a deal with Greece.

The Turkish-Cypriots have been let down by their compatriot Greek-Cypriots and by the international community. They were willing to compromise in 2004 to get a deal done but were rebuffed. They were led to believe that if they voted "yes" to the Annan plan and the Greek-Cypriots voted "no" that the EU and the international community would give them support and reduce their international isolation. That did not happen. When it came to Crans-Montana, they were again willing to compromise but were never taken seriously by Anastidiades. Mustafa Ergun Olgun correctly points out that "the Turkish-Cypriot people have been deprived of the right to exercise their political equality since 1963 and have been under economic, social and even sporting restrictions imposed by their former partners."[178]

Greek-Cypriots had several windows of their own to get to a favourable deal. This was certainly true in the mid-1960s, again in 2004, and once again most recently at Crans-Montana. But on each occasion the Greek-Cypriots never missed an opportunity to miss an opportunity. As Varnova and Faustmann point out in *Reunifying Cyprus,* "it is certainly possible to say that, in retrospect, each incarnation of settlement proposals has indeed been

---

178 Mustafa Ergun Olgun, "One Final Chance for Federalism," in *Resolving Cyprus,* ed. James Ker-Lindsay (London, I.B. Tauris, 2015), 214.

progressively worse for the Greek-Cypriots than those that came before."[179]

The same has often been said about the Palestinians. Somehow, they assumed that waiting would get them a better deal—but instead, the offers only got worse. We are sure that many moderate Palestinians wished they had cut a deal earlier when they witnessed President Trump and Prime Minister Netanyahu triumphantly outline their latest peace plan at the White House in January 2020. Likewise, the perfect time to get a deal done in Cyprus was in 2004 when the moons were virtually perfectly aligned. Alas, one moon was out of sync: the Greek-Cypriot leadership under President Papadopoulos.

Historical animosity, political gamesmanship, greed, and grave misjudgements have all contributed to Greek-Cypriot intransigence. It is interesting to note that the literal Greek translation for "give and take" is "take and give." All take with little give has led to this impasse. The end result is no solution: a bad outcome for both Greek-Cypriots and Turkish-Cypriots and increased tension within NATO and between Turkey and the United States and Western Europe.

In many ways the Cyprus situation is analogous to a marriage that has run its course. As we pointed out in the last chapter, many harsh words have been hurled in anger over the years, and the two parties do not trust each other. It is hard to build a marriage without trust. We are now left with a situation in which the parties

179 Varnova and Faustmann, *Reunifying Cyprus*, 19.

share a house because they cannot afford to move out. They cannot agree on terms of a divorce settlement, or on terms to get back together. After many years of living on different floors of the same house, they are extremely unhappy. They cannot use the beautiful communal garden of the house and they won't let each other see the kids. The only prudent and realistic option is to negotiate a divorce. They could then divide their assets, see the kids, and enjoy their separate lives.

This same scenario is true for Cyprus. Greek-Cypriots take great pleasure in knowing that the north is still isolated and recognized by no one but Turkey. They revel in the knowledge that the north cannot trade freely with the world and, given this isolation, that the Cypriots in the north are less well off than they are. But how does holding Turkish-Cypriots down help Greek-Cypriots in any way? It does not. Bringing grief and pain to the other side does not bring increased happiness to your side. It only guarantees that more scar tissue is created. Having a difficult and tense relationship with Turkey—a much stronger adversary, only forty miles away—does not seem promising.

This has gone on far too long. Both sides would be better off than they are under the status quo if they negotiated a velvet divorce. Business schools teach the concept of BATNA (the Best Alternative to a Negotiated Agreement). The optimal outcome in Cyprus would be a negotiated agreement to re-establish one country under a BZBC framework. But if that cannot be achieved, which we strongly believe to be the case, then a velvet divorce is the best alternative to such a negotiated agreement. Division is not meant to be salvific: it is meant to find a solution that will allow the two parties to live a more prosperous and peaceful life than they can today. If it comes to this, the majority in Cyprus must be willing, after sixty years of failing to find a solution, to let the minority live their lives peacefully, with the chance to pursue its own prosperity and happiness. If a BZBC deal is not possible, then the world must recognize Turkish-Cypriots. The EU brought peace to the former Yugoslavia by recognizing distinct ethnic groups and nations. They owe the same to Turkish-Cypriots.

Living harmoniously will not occur overnight. As TRNC Foreign Minister Ozersay told us in his office in Nicosia: "We need to go one step at a time. The EU did not start as the EU. It started with coal and steel and then evolved into a single market and then a single currency." The same step-by-step process will need to be followed to ensure that the two nations can peacefully share the same small island.

If our book has made at least one point very clear, the strategy of kicking the can down the road is fraught with danger. Partition exists today. As each year goes by, partition becomes more permanent and almost impossible to knock down. If the Greek-Cypriots wait too much longer to compromise, they will end up negotiating with Turkey instead of the Turkish-Cypriots. Greek-Cypriots do not want to have a Turkish province on their island but this is exactly what they will get. Once that happens, it may be that a deal is never possible. That is why it is in the south's best interest to negotiate a velvet divorce now while they still have someone to negotiate with, and they still have some leverage. Greek-Cypriots will probably object to a more formal partition arguing that this gives the Turkish-Cypriots exactly what they have wanted all along but this is provably false. The Turkish-Cypriots voted overwhelmingly to rejoin their countrymen in a united Cyprus in the 2004 referendum but this re-unification was soundly rejected by the Greek-Cypriots.

This is certainly a case where the perfect is the enemy of the good. Both sides need to understand that the world is not as they would wish. Cypriots have been told what to do by outsiders for thousands of years. Now it is time for them to control their own destiny. If Germany and France, after centuries of war where millions died, can forget the past and build a strong coalition, surely the Greek-Cypriots and Turkish-Cypriots can do the same. This can either be together in a BZBC nation or as two peaceful nations co-existing on the same island. Realists on both sides need to take over from the dreamers who ask for it all and make matters worse.

BZBC would be a wonderful outcome, however unlikely. A velvet divorce, the probable outcome, would at least be preferable to the status quo and the unpromising future that will attend inaction. It would permit positive exchanges between the two nations sharing the island and allow each to forge a better future. But time is running out.

ACKNOWLEDGEMENTS

THIS BOOK HAS BEEN in the works for the past two decades. My two tours peacekeeping in Cyprus some forty plus years ago led to my initial fascination with this spectacular island. Many of the soldiers I served with on those tours were great resources for us as we developed this book. To them and to all the peacekeepers around the world we wan to offer our sincere thanks for their help and for their service.

The foundation for this book was the year-long study that I undertook for my thesis at the Sorbonne twenty years ago. One person in particular was instrumental in introducing me back then and again over the past few years to senior politicians, ambassadors and diplomats. We met Berna Huebner during our year in Paris and she tirelessly connected us with people in Cyprus, London, Brussels and the US.

We also want to acknowledge and thank the politicians on both sides of the Green Line in Cyprus who made time available to us to respond to our many questions. We were also given great access to key players in London and in Brussels at the EU who offered valuable insights into the challenges that the EU faced admitting

Cyprus to the club. Many of these folks preferred to remain anonymous so that they could share their true perspectives rather than recite the "talking points". Their honesty and transparency help guide us as we did our research for this book.

The perspective of academics such as Professor Hubert Faustmann of the University of Cyprus and Dr Ahmet Sozen, Chair of the Department of Political Science and International Relations at Eastern Mediterranean University in Cyprus and James Ker-Lindsay of the London School of Economics in London was instrumental in providing us with the institutional knowledge about the many failed attempts to bring the two ethnic parties together in Cyprus.

We would also thank the senior politicians who have followed the Cyprus file closely over the years and could provide an objective point-of-view. This included former UK Foreign Secretary, Jack Straw, who graciously hosted us at his home in London. Former US Ambassador to Cyprus John Koenig was a key source as he was willing during his time in Cyprus to challenge the status quo. Lord David Hannay, Baron of Chiswick, had strong views backed up by many years of experience in Cyprus. Lord Hannay played a vital role in the key years of 1996 to 2003 as the UN Special Representative for Cyprus. The former Australian Minister of Foreign Affairs Alexander Downer, who served as the UN envoy to Cyprus for six years provided the unique perspective of an experienced politician and diplomat who had also tried to bring peace to Cyprus.

We were fortunate to spend some 90 minutes interviewing Rauf Denktash in his office back in 2002. He was the father of the

Turkish Republic of North Cyprus and he had strong views on every topic. He was a hardliner who had endured discrimination and aggression in his native land and was a firm believer that the two communities could only come together if the Greek-Cypriots were willing to compromise which he felt they were not prepared to do. He correctly predicted that the Greek-Cypriots would enter the EU on their own even though this was a violation of international law.

We would also like to thank my wife and my co-author's Mom, Pamela Stevenson, who listened to our many discussions on this topic for several years and provided us with valuable feedback which strongly influenced the final version of the book.

Finally and most importantly we would thank our editor, Ken Whyte. Ken was a master at simplifying a complex story and he challenged us when our arguments were weak or when we strayed from the main thesis. He was curious about Cyprus and brought years of experience in helping us mold the final product.